Come On Home warmed my heart from the start and left me inspired—to be a more intentional mom and a better daughter, and to cherish every bit of family God has given me. This book is packed with heartwarming stories, sage advice, and some of the very best resource lists! I think this may be the only family/parenting book you need—and that says a lot, since I've written a few myself! What a gift *Come On Home* will be to the world!

MONICA SWANSON, host of the *Monica Swanson Podcast* and author of *Boy Mom*, *Raising Amazing*, and *Becoming Homeschoolers*

Come On Home invites parents to nurture the kind of homes their children will want to return to someday. With delightful personal stories, biblical insight, and plenty of practical ideas, Jessica Smartt has provided a trusted guide for fostering unshakable bonds that will pull a family together even when the world seeks to tear them apart.

JAMIE ERICKSON, author of *Holy Hygge* and founder of the Biblio-files

In a world that pulls families apart, *Come On Home* guides us together again. Jessica Smartt reminds us that home is where we are known, loved, and truly belong. The insights and reminders in this book will inspire you to build a family culture that reflects grace, joy, and love while discarding anything less.

RACHEL WOJO, wife and mom to six, author of *Desperate Prayers* and *One More Step*

In *Come On Home*, Jessica Smartt offers a refreshing and grace-filled approach to building a strong, loving family. With practical wisdom, heartfelt stories, and biblical truth, she reminds us that creating a close-knit home is both possible and deeply impactful. As a wife, mother, and fellow believer, I found her insights to be encouraging and transformative. This book is a must-read for anyone longing to cultivate a family that not only loves but truly enjoys one another.

RACHAEL ADAMS, author of *Everyday Prayers for Love* and host of *The Love Offering* podcast

Come On Home is a witty, honest treasure trove of experience, godly insight, and practical ideas that invite a group of people who happen to be in a house to become a "family with a home." The book threads the balance between nurturing your kid's God-given dignity and their need for tough love. It's refreshingly honest about the fatigue and confusion of parenting, yet somehow you are left feeling a kind of inspired courage.

ROGER EDWARDS, therapist and father of seven

If you're looking for a relatable, practical, and encouraging motherhood book, *Come On Home* is it. As I read Jessica's words, it felt like I was having a conversation with a good friend. The experiences she shares about raising her family are inspiring, and the ideas she gives to prioritize what really matters are wonderful and doable. I've both laughed and cried as I read her words on building a strong family because I was so inspired and motivated to mirror her ideas in my own family. A must-read for every mother no matter what season of life they're in.

MACKENZIE WILCOX, homeschool mom and writer @twigsandsage

Come On Home is an incredible look at what it takes to be a strong Christ-centered family in this ever-changing world. With a perfect blend of practical applications and a strong call to steward our homes well, I was inspired and convicted as I read each page.

ASHLEE WILLIAMS, Grace and Grit homeschooling content creator

Jessica Smartt's words are wise and encouraging, providing the practical truth families need to intentionally grow a firm foundation. But the best part is that she doesn't pretend to have it all together (who does?). Instead, she paints a vision of what can be (and why it matters) and offers practical steps to get there. The concepts in *Come On Home* matter deeply for the world we are leaving our children. It's that important.

BROOKE McGLOTHLIN, mom of two and author of *Praying for Teen Boys*

Come On Home

TYNDALE
MOMENTUM®

A Tyndale nonfiction imprint

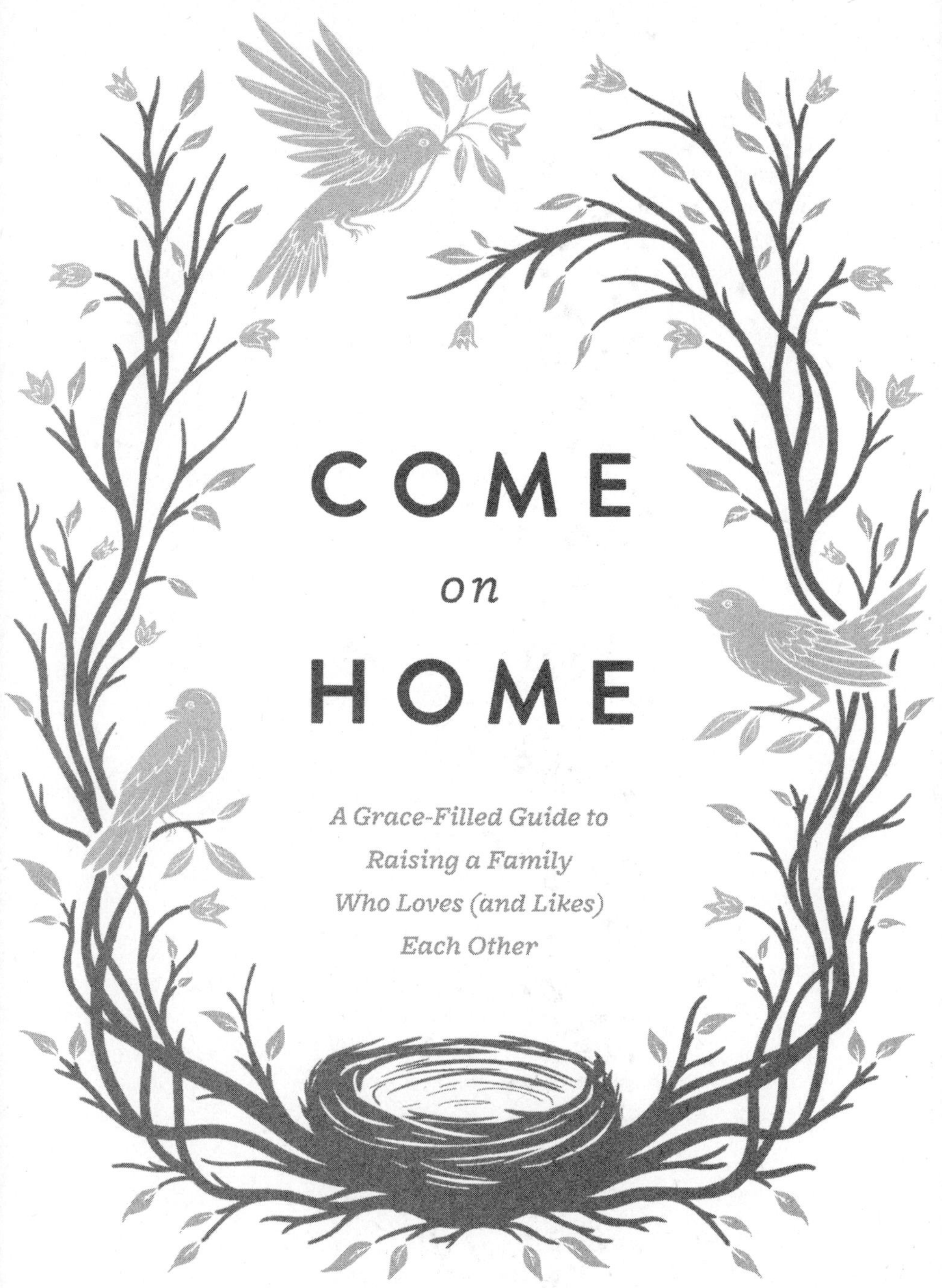

COME *on* HOME

A Grace-Filled Guide to Raising a Family Who Loves (and Likes) Each Other

JESSICA SMARTT

Visit Tyndale online at tyndale.com.

Visit Tyndale Momentum online at tyndalemomentum.com.

Tyndale, Tyndale's quill logo, *Tyndale Momentum*, and the Tyndale Momentum logo are registered trademarks of Tyndale House Ministries. Tyndale Momentum is a nonfiction imprint of Tyndale House Publishers, Carol Stream, Illinois.

Come On Home: A Grace-Filled Guide to Raising a Family Who Loves (and Likes) Each Other

Copyright © 2025 by Jessica Smartt. All rights reserved.

Cover illustration of nest and branches by Sarah Susan Richardson. Copyright © Tyndale House Ministries. All rights reserved.

Cover illustration of birds copyright © Rudzhan/Adobe Stock. All rights reserved.

Author photograph copyright © 2024 by Jacquelyn Ragan. All rights reserved.

Cover design by Libby Dykstra

Interior design by Cathy Miller

Edited by Donna L. Berg

Published in association with the literary agency of Mary DeMuth Literary.

Unless otherwise indicated, all Scripture quotations are taken from the Holy Bible, *New International Version,® NIV.®* Copyright © 1973, 1978, 1984, 2011 by Biblica, Inc.® Used by permission. All rights reserved worldwide.

Scripture quotations marked ESV are from The ESV® Bible (The Holy Bible, English Standard Version®), copyright © 2001 by Crossway, a publishing ministry of Good News Publishers. Used by permission. All rights reserved.

Scripture quotations marked NKJV are taken from the New King James Version,® copyright © 1982 by Thomas Nelson. Used by permission. All rights reserved.

Some of the anecdotal illustrations in this book are true to life and are included with the permission of the persons involved. Names and some details have been changed to protect privacy. All other illustrations are composites of real situations, and any resemblance to people living or dead is purely coincidental.

For information about special discounts for bulk purchases, please contact Tyndale House Publishers at csresponse@tyndale.com, or call 1-855-277-9400.

Library of Congress Cataloging-in-Publication Data

A catalog record for this book is available from the Library of Congress.

ISBN 979-8-4005-0482-2

Printed in the United States of America

31 30 29 28 27 26 25
7 6 5 4 3 2 1

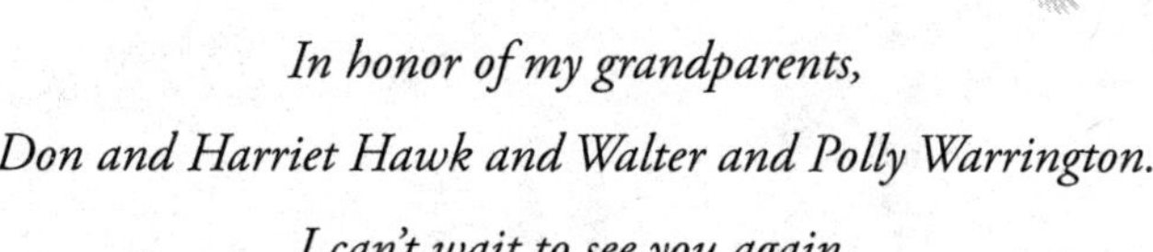

In honor of my grandparents,

Don and Harriet Hawk and Walter and Polly Warrington.

I can't wait to see you again.

Contents

A Note from Jessica

Dear sweet reader,

Before you jump into this book, there are a few things I want you to know.

Strong family is not only a passion of mine but a gift I have received. I live on a family compound with eighteen family members, for crying out loud. Excepting a few aggressive roosters, no one has been murdered. For the most part, we genuinely enjoy spending time together. Same with my husband's family (minus the compound and the murdered roosters). We hold this rare treasure of close-knit, healthy families with thankful hands.

But also: our family is still in process. I have kids who fight—not subtly, with friendly pokes under the dinner table, but loudly, with blood drawn. I am right here with you, raising normal kids. I'm not writing this as a gray-haired, seventy-year-old grandma, passing down my infallible, repeatable formula for family togetherness. I'm walking alongside you—as hungry as you are for wise voices, for practical ideas to sink our teeth into. I wrote this book because I needed it too.

I know that family is tricky. I know that you face your own specific challenges as you raise your family. I don't pretend that your family looks like my family, or your life looks like my life. While I would love to help equip you for every possible scenario, I can't do that in the scope of this book. What I have done instead is to offer general principles so you can flesh them out in your particular situation. I have tried my best to be nuanced, sensitive, and careful with my wording. I hope this comes through.

Next, while this book is about raising strong families, I'll primarily be talking to moms, since I am one.

One more thing: I am a Christian. If this is not a faith you share, I want you to know two things. One, I am so, so grateful that you have chosen to pick up this book. I see the value in having people around me with different opinions and different voices. My heart is that you would not feel "on the outside" but would receive my own experience with the measure of grace with which it is intended. Two, I hope (and know!) that you will receive much inspiration from this book as you seek to raise your own strong family.

Oh, and one last thing. If you're like me, thinking about all this strong family stuff might make you feel things. Things like:

I messed up there.

Missed the boat on that.

It's too late.

All moms—all good moms—struggle with self-doubt, past guilt, and parenting fails. *Don't let it get to you.* Here is the truth. Hold on to this, okay?

You are the right mom for your kids.

It's never too late.

You aren't alone.

Love,
Jessica

PS: I would love to hear from you. You can email me at jessicasmartt@gmail.com.

INTRODUCTION

LEGACY

How Moms Can Change the World

October 4, 2021.

Two weeks from Grammy's ninety-third birthday. Six of us huddled around her bed.

There are so many details I can't forget. The crackling rattle in her labored breathing, each breath so unnaturally far from the last one. My sister on the other side of the bed, so strong, singing hymns. Her voice wavered and caught, but she kept singing, distinctly and loudly.

I was not sure when it happened. Her breaths were minutes apart. When was she gone? When was she here? We told her she could go, that we would be okay. We realized she was crying—eyes glassy, distant, fixed on nothing—but somehow we knew she had heard.

In the final minutes, my dad spoke familiar, comforting words over her. "In My Father's house are many mansions; if it were not so, I would have told you. I go to prepare a place for you. And if I go and prepare a place for you, I will come again and receive you to Myself; that where I am, there you may be also."[1]

It was a holy room, full of sorrow and hope, aching and beauty . . . and so much love.

She was dearly loved. I don't want to die, but I do want to die like that.

Ninety pounds with a handful of sweaters to her name when she died. But Grammy? She was the richest, whole-est person I have ever met. She built a legacy.

> *legacy:* the long-term impact of the events or actions in a person's life.[2]

To use the word *legacy* feels so cliché, imperfect. How can I explain what she left? What she did?

Seven children, twenty-one grandchildren, thirty-six great-grandchildren. Every single one of them knew they were loved by Grammy.

One time Grammy was going to the store. "Do you need anything?" she asked me with her beautiful smile. "Oh, yes, some potato chips, some pretzels, some ice cream, some candy . . ." It was a lame attempt at a joke from a nine-year-old.

She came back an hour later, saying, "I think I got it all!" I felt terrible, and terribly loved. She lived meagerly, spent all she had on us. Always on us. Her double-wide was the house of canned peaches and Schwan's pizzas and perfectly layered macaroni and cheese and Push Pops and *Country* magazine and the old awful couches where we made so many memories.

Grammy made home. She defined it. Her life was spent at the kitchen sink and the stove. She poured hours into loving people with sausage, eggs, and Folgers coffee. She gave us a rich, rich life.

I want this kind of legacy. Her life was not wasted.

One time my husband told my mom, "Thank you for loving Jessica so well. You loved her well, and now she can love well." My mom was loved, and she loved, and I can love. It has been legacies of love.

Of all my privileges, the most profound is the gift of family to propel me into life. I'm closer to my aunts than some are to their mothers. I'm closer with my cousins than many are with their siblings. We gather still, hordes of us, in a big living room, bringing our pasta salad and baked beans and babies in car seats and teenagers in hoodies, drinking tea and playing music late into the night. Cousins, grandparents, uncles, aunts, sisters, in-laws and "out-laws" (as my dad jokingly calls his sons-in-law)—and there are always one or two extras who didn't have anywhere to go, anything to do. This kind of family is magnetic, compelling, loud, and messy in the very best way.

WHAT IS A STRONG FAMILY?

I imagine you reading this now. Are you crying with me? Grammy is an inspiration to those of us who hold a deep desire to be intentional with the ones God's entrusted us with, to build a lasting legacy of love and faith.

But if you aren't crying, maybe you're mad. Because maybe this all feels foreign, impossible. Family is so messy, so terribly specific and practical. You wonder if you have what it takes to break the cycle, to overcome the challenges in your circumstance to give your kids a different legacy. If that's what you're bringing to this book, I see you. And I want you to know: *family doesn't have to be perfect to be strong.*

I often draw deep strength from thinking about my Grammy as

a young mom. Her husband was a traveling, amusing-but-mostly-absent man. She had no support system and moved thirty-four times in her marriage. They were so poor my Grammy would cook dandelion soup and cow tongue for dinner for her little ones. There was nothing else to make. She struggled with health issues. Although we grandkids joked that she "never sinned," she assuredly was human and did not parent perfectly. Despite all this, what a legacy she built!

You and I each come to this book with our own ideas of what a "strong family" is.

Maybe we unconsciously picture this perpetually cheerful family, the perfect marriage—no big blowups, minimal stress, everyone magically agreeing about everything and being thrilled to spend time together.

Fortunately, that is not it. The really wonderful news is this: a strong family is not about perfection but *grace*.

A strong family is not about superficial harmony but *deep friendship*.

A strong family is not about physical proximity but *unshakable loyalty*.

One of the things my mom would often say to us over the years is this: "Come on home, and then we'll figure it out." Maybe one of us had had a frustrating day, felt bogged down by unresolved problems or unsettling conversations. "Just come on home," she'd say. "We'll figure it out."

Come on home.

Home is the place you can go when you don't have the answer.

Home is the place you can laugh through the tears, rest when you're weary, hunker down when you've made a mess of things.

Home is the place where you're loved, where you're safe.

This kind of home, this kind of family is powerful.

The truth? Strong families like this will save the world.

THE POWER OF CLOSE-KNIT FAMILIES

You might be thinking, *Strong families are important, but to say they will "save the world"? Is that true?*

Yes, and here's why.

Kids with good roots can hold up in the world and hold the world up.

A strong family undergirds you with strength to face whatever comes. I love how child psychologist Kim John Payne puts it: a strong family offers "a place to retreat to, to restock, restore, to repair . . . and to prepare for going out into those bumpy seas." It's a "safe harbor" that fills us and heals us to go back out into that harsh and difficult world. When we create strong families, he muses, we get a kid who can say, "I know I'm alone in the playground, but I don't have to be alone in my life. I've got my family."[3]

Strong family grounds you, and also launches you out to change the world. Whether our kids are meant to be teachers, programmers, entrepreneurs, nurses, or pastors, *kids who are undergirded by a strong family can take risks, love well, make mistakes, try again*. Additionally, they just might save thousands of dollars and so many years *not* unpacking their deep-seated family traumas in therapy sessions. (I mean, let's be honest, my kids will probably still have some therapy, but hopefully less?)

THE JOURNEY AHEAD

In the rest of this book, we will unpack what a close-knit, healthy family really looks like. Uncovering research, stories, and ideas, we will go behind the metal doors to see "how the sausage is made," sparing no corner of insight to reveal the recipe.

First, we will look at the *foundation* for a close-knit family, or what a family needs to grow strong. You know how in college certain courses have prerequisites? The characteristics we'll explore are sort of the "prerequisites" for building a strong family. Of course, the college analogy breaks down a bit, because unlike when you take a class and you're done, these foundational elements are a process throughout our lives! You might have noticed the chapter topics for part 1: *honesty*, *perspective*, *authority*, *partnership*, and *prayer*. Those words might feel a little abstract, but this "get ready" section will be anything but bland, as we cover mom self-care, keeping the marriage spark alive, side gigs, miraculous answers to prayer, and the ideal kind of parenting: "elephant parenting." (Intrigued about that one? Stay tuned!)

In part 2, we will look at the *picture* of a strong family, or how a strong family looks as it grows. We will unpack eight key characteristics of close-knit families: *time*, *connection*, *memories*, *nest*, *roots*, *loyalty*, *friendship*, and *grace*. This is where we will get down to the nitty-gritty, with all those ideas, resources, and examples you're hoping for. Every so often, I've "given the mic" to some amazing parents I know and respect—from all different kinds of families—to share their stories.

This book is *packed* with ideas, stories, and examples—things I've learned or observed in strong families. But of course, these are ultimately suggestions. No one could do all of this; some of it may not fit for your family. Don't feel pressured or overwhelmed. Take what's helpful; leave what's not.

I want to make you two promises for this journey.

First promise. The principles I will share are things that anyone can implement. You don't have to have a lot of money. You don't have to have great examples. Maybe you're a widowed mom, a divorced mom, a mom with a blended family. Maybe you're raising children with special needs. I know that your life and your parenting represent some unique challenges. My hope and prayer is that these foundational principles will be relevant and life-giving to you—*no matter where you are or what your situation.*

Second promise. While building a family will feel hard at times, it will be worth it. Because after all, here is what you do when you give your kids a strong family:

- You tether them to something solid in a changing world.
- You give them friends, people who are really and truly behind them.
- You give them memories, good ones, to draw from in dark and lonely times.
- You give them a soft place to land.
- You give them theology that is Velveteen Rabbit–real, with skin and bones.
- You build a healthy society, because healthy families build healthy people build healthy cultures.
- In building a legacy, you are changing the very tint of time.

Some of us in this race are handed the baton by others running behind us. It is our job to hold on to it and keep running.

Some of us *start* the relay. We must pick up that baton and take the first step.

Someone has to start the race. There is always a person who starts.

For me, it was Grammy.

Look at your life. Has someone else started the race for your family? Or will it be you? Can it be you?

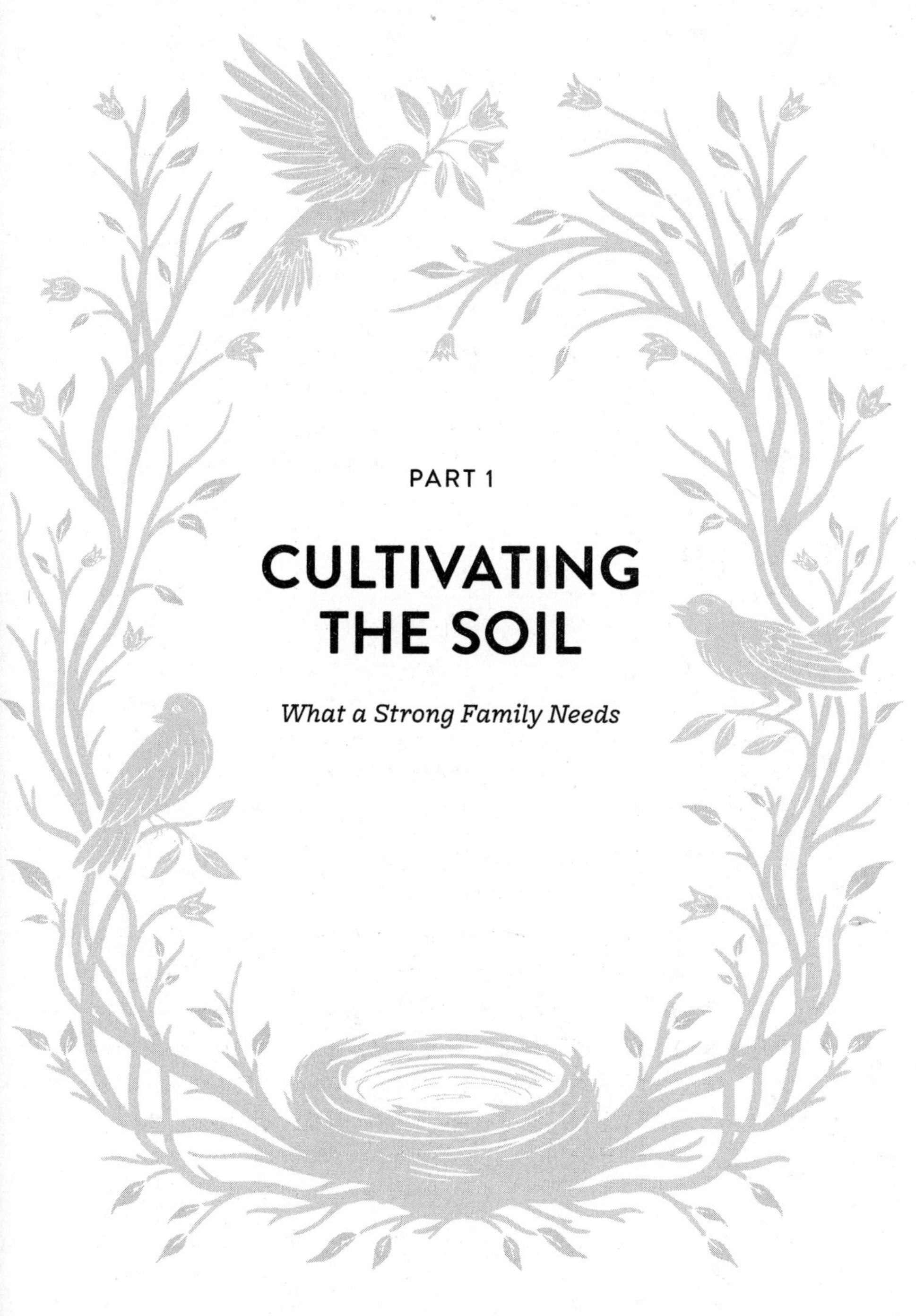

PART 1

CULTIVATING THE SOIL

What a Strong Family Needs

1

HONESTY

Admit Where You Are to Build What You Want

Honesty is often very hard. The truth is often painful. But the freedom it can bring is worth the trying.

FRED ROGERS

"If we're going to medicate you, I want to *medicate* you."

I am sitting on a cold, blue plastic chair. It is May outside, but nothing feels warm or full of light in this sterile OB office with the beady-eyed doctor. My mom is nodding. It feels like I am not here, have lost all say in my life.

But this loss of autonomy is necessary. They are worried.

I am crying constantly. I don't like being a mom. Two weeks in, and I feel madly deceived. Why, I wonder, does everyone throw showers for this? Why did I get those glittery blue-sparkle Hallmark cards that said "Congratulations!"?

Congratulations for what, I wonder? If everyone thinks this is wonderful, then clearly something is off with me. How could I have been so horribly wrong all my life, when all I longed for was to be a mother? How could this be my calling if I am so terrible at it?

Such were my first experiences as a mother. I thought I would be the world's most amazing mom, and then I actually became one. We moved into my parents' house for three weeks because I was unraveling at the seams. It was a crushing embarrassment.

It was during this season that I began seeing a kind, old counselor. I confessed it all—how I was failing, how no other moms I knew seemed to be struggling like I was. He was quiet for a minute, then looked at me with soft eyes, a twinkle hiding behind them, and said the words I will remember for the rest of my life: "I think if anyone says they love poop, they are lying."

We had a good long laugh.

When I look back, I'm impressed with the genius of his counseling. Laughing was something I hadn't done in a month. Knowing that he, too, hated the smell of poop was weirdly reassuring. And he gave me permission to be honest. Slowly, I began to grow.

I absolutely love being a mother now. I would not say I am the world's *best* mother, but even on the bleakest of days, we haven't had to resort to living in my parents' guest room, so I would say that is a win. The fact that I adore being a mom and am writing this book is a true testimony to the miracles that God is able to do.

Being honest about my struggles was the first step. Once I said it out loud, admitted the state I was in, and asked for help, I began to heal.

HOW YOU ARE DOING MATTERS

Fortunately, the state of things in *your* life isn't likely to be as bleak as it was for me in those first weeks of motherhood. But the truth remains: the first step to improving anything is being honest. *Before you can have the family you want, you have to get real about the family you have.* In this chapter, we are going to do an honest inventory in which we'll cover four aspects of *you*, the mom: capacity, health, gifts, and weaknesses. With these honest assessments, you'll be able to see where you're thriving and where you're merely surviving, and then you'll be empowered to make choices that set the tone you want for your family.

To have a great family, you have to realize that YOU (the mom) are the one who affects things the most in the family. This may be a bit controversial, but based on my experience and years of study, I believe that a mother is the single greatest influence in a family, for bad or for good. In *Habits for a Sacred Home*, Jennifer Pepito shares that during a rough patch of motherhood, her dad told her, "You are the cheerleader of this operation, and if you are down, everyone is down."[1]

Moms are active, not passive. We set the tone. It has been a decade and a half of embracing the fact that as a mother, I am a thermostat and not a thermometer. As I am not a science-y person, I have to think about the difference between these two for a minute: a thermostat sets the temperature; a thermometer reads it. As mothers, we aren't reading the room, we are controlling it.

If you are like me, this makes you feel a little stressed out. It is a big responsibility we carry. But it is also exciting. You are not powerless. You are powerful!

GETTING REAL ABOUT YOUR *CAPACITY*

To me, one of the most frustrating things about life is that we can't do everything. I tried, and I can tell you the exact moment that I realized we cannot. It was a Thursday afternoon in June, and I was lying on the couch, withering away in life. Cause of death: Summer VBS. I fell asleep smack-dab in the middle of the living room, with three little kids doing who knows what all around the house. I woke up once and remember thinking I could not lift my arms. It was like a giant monster was sitting on top of me. Since I have hypochondria, there were sundry explanations for my coma-like state, most involving tumors and blood disorders.

It took a very good friend to say it: "Jessica. You are doing way too much. You need to stop." I was homeschooling two kids while I had a very busy toddler. I was making all our food from scratch because my son has multiple life-threatening food allergies. (I'll tell you more about this in chapter 5.) I had taken on a position as children's ministry director, and not content to merely organize VBS, I decided to be the head Bible teacher, the MC, and in one final hurrah of micromanaging, to make all the hot dogs for the cookout. WHAT WAS I THINKING?

This was a truly shocking epiphany: my capacity is limited! I have to be choosy. There is so much I *could* do, but that does not mean I should do it all. I would love to say that I got up from the couch, quit children's ministry, and never made this mistake again. Unfortunately, only two of those three things happened. My adult life has been a constant dance: get way overwhelmed with my commitments, quit them, and repeat. I am a slow learner. But I am learning. Each breakdown gives me yet another tool to tuck away for the next season of overwhelm.

Another pivotal moment happened five years later, when I was ten thousand feet in the air on the way to San Diego for one of my son's allergy treatments. I was reading the book *Essentialism* in seat 16B. In it the author encourages readers to choose only what is essential in life and eliminate the rest. "I can do anything but not everything," he says.[2]

I had a hunch that I wasn't exactly living by this wisdom and that maybe it was the source of the ball of stress I was carrying constantly. I made a list of all the things I was doing. So many things. Too many things. Have you recently made a list of all the things you do? One question the author asks is, if this commitment or opportunity were not on your plate, how hard would you work to obtain it?[3] I realized how many things I was doing not because I really wanted to do them but because I didn't want to do the work of off-loading them. I mentally took all the things off of my plate and then added back only the things that were truly essential, that only I could do. I was left with a delightfully doable list.

My fear is that you would walk away from this book burdened and overwhelmed. *What I want you to see is what a gift you could give yourself.* This moment, right now, wherever you are—whether you are glasses-on, sleepy-eyed in bed, or scrounging a few free minutes while the kids swim in the plastic pool—this is your chance. Maybe this is the answer to that low-lying guilt or overwhelm you've been carrying for so long.

I encourage you to take a minute right now and list everything you do.

You probably just read that sentence and didn't do what I recommended, right? Because that is what I usually do when I am reading a book. But I beg you to do it. This little exercise was one of the most powerful things I have done in the past five years. Trust me? Get up from that comfy spot and grab a pencil. You'll find some space at the end of this chapter to write down your list of responsibilities.

Now. Read over your list. There is too much on your plate, maybe. Perhaps that is why you are so tired, so overwhelmed?

Clean off that plate. What should remain are the things that only *you* can do. You are a limited You. Your bucket is only so big, and your days only so many. Are you doing what you truly want? We mothers are intuitively really good at knowing the answer to that question, if we would only take a minute to listen to ourselves. What is your gut telling you?

GETTING REAL ABOUT YOUR *HEALTH*

Maybe when you read this subhead you were thinking *physical* health, like the inexplicable fatigue you're constantly seeking the cause of. (Hint: it's children. The cause is children.) My definition of health here is not less than that, but more. What I mean is, *Are you thriving?* We need you to be the *best* You that you can possibly be. How are you doing? This building-a-strong-family thing is a marathon, not a sprint. Is your pace sustainable? Do you have injuries (literal or figurative) that you need to stop and deal with?

Think back to my thermostat versus thermometer example. People who are maintaining the "temperature" for the whole house have a big job. It's a great idea to build a strong family, but maybe you need to take a minute and deal with a few things. Do you need counseling for past trauma? I'm sorry for such an un-fun sentence, but these sorts of things do not get better by sitting untouched for a few decades. What about your marriage? Could it use some attention? (More on that in chapter 4.) Or if you're a single mom, are you finding time for friendships that nourish your soul? Has it been years since you've had your blood work done and you're hobbling through life? Whatever it is, maybe you've been waiting for a sign to deal with "that thing." Here is your sign, mama!

Sometimes these are hard questions to answer well for yourself. We are all skewed to see things a little bit wrong when it comes to our own needs. To get a really good answer, ask someone who knows and loves you well. Maybe your husband? Say something like "What's one thing you wish I would do to take better care of myself?" I dare you to ask.

Growing a strong family takes work, and work wears you down. I struggle with navigating the balance of caring for myself and caring for my family. Sometimes I look at other moms, like my sister Jenny, and am so convicted by how they pour out their lives for their families. I feel like a lazy bum compared to them. I have friends who exude cheerfulness and peace. I wonder if it is because they are so wise in implementing life-giving rhythms. I feel convicted that in my hurried busyness I don't care for myself well enough and the stress bleeds into my family. What is the right balance? How do you care for yourself well—but not *too* well, you know?

Obviously, there's no one-size-fits-all answer, but God gave me a vision recently that might be as helpful to you as it has been to me. I should note that I'm a Presbyterian and therefore don't get these "vision" sort of moments too often, so don't get worried I'm going off the deep end. I'm going to throw a few different word pictures at you. My mom would use visual metaphors when I was growing up to teach me lessons, and I hated it, and now I have turned into her.

The first vision was of me. As I write this, it is the end of a homeschool school year, and I am parched for rest. God showed me, "Jessica, this is what you are like." The image was of my nephew, Tommy, when he was learning to juggle. He would dive one direction, dip the other, drop one tennis ball, and frantically toss up another one. This is what I am doing, only instead of tennis balls, it is like I am juggling eggs—raw eggs—and way too many of them. If I drop one, it will go crashing to the floor, totally destroyed. It is a desperate, unsustainable dance.

And then my mind flashed to a different image. A peaceful one. I saw, in my mind's eye, one of our hens sitting on her nest, patiently, calmly, carefully brooding over her precious eggs. I feel like God was telling me, "Those eggs you think you're juggling—you're not actually in control. But I've got them. They are in my loving care. Rest and relax."

I wasn't made for juggling a dozen uncooked eggs. I can only hold two things, really, one in each hand. *Love the Lord your God with all your heart, and all your soul, and all your mind, and all your strength* (that's one thing), and *love your neighbor as yourself* (that's the other thing).[4] Those are my priorities. That is the job God has given me.

And that's our job as mothers as we take care of ourselves and our families—to love God, love others. Our job is to hold those two "eggs" as we walk through this marathon of life. We fulfill our calling from God to love others well (that's our families too!), and then we leave the results to Him.

Godly self-care is what helps you do that job well. If I stop and get a good night's sleep, I can do my job better. If I spend time in prayer, I can do my job better. If I get away once in a while with my husband and sleep in, eat yummy food, and hike in nature, I can come home and do that job better.

On the other hand, if my self-care distracts me from loving others well, that might not be ideal. If my self-care has me thriving, but my kids or my husband are struggling, I may need to consider whether I've gone too far the other way. Good self-care strengthens us to do our work. And let's not forget, our work as mothers is a God-given assignment! We are to raise these kids well, to the glory of God and for the good of the Kingdom. We love Him and we love others.

How are you doing with those eggs? Are you holding the right things? Are you feeling the stress of juggling things you weren't meant to juggle? Are you taking care of yourself on this walk of motherhood? Are you healthy? Is there a wound that you need to pay attention to?

When I was in the thick of raising little kids, I learned something about self-care that might be helpful to you if you're in a similar season. I treasure the memories of these years, but gosh, at the time, it often felt like I was trapped in the house perpetually. At one point, Todd and I finagled a way to escape to a resort across town for a few nights. It was heavenly. I ordered the luxurious crab cake Benedict every morning because why would you not? One morning we biked across town, and I remember feeling a bit depressed that this vacation would soon be over. *How can I carry the spirit of this back with me into my normal life?* I wondered as I pedaled. The thought came to me, *I can't. But what would be magic is if I could create little happy moments in my day to recharge . . . while being with the kids.*

If you're in a season where it's hard to get away for large chunks of time, can you think of ways to recharge *with* your family? This is a tricky sort of math equation, because kids are exhausting and don't perhaps naturally share your hobbies. But it is worth brainstorming. Because if you could think of things that fill your cup AND build a strong family—wouldn't that be gold? See the list of "Self-Care Activities *with Kids*" for a few ideas I came up with. Some of these might sound terrible to you, but maybe the list will get you started. Now obviously, any of these scenarios have the capacity to crash and burn entirely if someone suddenly has a meltdown. Meltdowns are not restful. Amen.

Self-Care Activities *with Kids*

- Sit on a blanket and read while your kids play at the park.
- Take nature walks together.
- Plan a girls' trip with your daughter.
- Take your son on an overnight to a fancy hotel for a significant birthday. (My friend does this—she gets to "wine and dine," and her son lives it up in the pool.)
- Get away with your husband.
- Take your daughter with you to a bridal or baby shower.
- Take a kid to Costco. (You get an extra hand for boxes; they get free samples. One child of mine still talks about his fifteen minutes in the sample massage chair.)
- You run while your child rollerblades. (Recommended only with experienced rollerbladers. Not beginners.)

GETTING REAL ABOUT YOUR *GIFTS*

One thing that is cool is that I am not you. We are different. Maybe wildly different. Maybe you are the kind of girl who forgets to eat lunch, for example, or some other inconceivable quirk. As you seek to raise a strong family, your unique traits and gifts can be used strategically. In fact, God made you just the way you are for a reason. As we launch into building this strong family, I encourage you to personalize your approach. You are equipped—just as you are—to be an amazing mom.

It might not always feel that way. Something I haven't mentioned yet is that I struggle with OCD and anxiety—yet God picked me to parent a child with life-threatening allergies! Do you find this as funny as I do? At first glance, doesn't it feel wrong? A mistake? I said so to my pastor, and I will never forget what he told me. "Honestly, Jessica, I think God made a perfect choice. If I were God, I think that is exactly the kind of mother I would want for a child like that. You are smart. You pay attention. You are careful. God knew exactly what He was doing." This flip-flop to my thinking has carried me through many dark times. I am uniquely gifted for parenting my son.

As you frame your family's culture, you will need every last ounce of your unique giftings. Who you are is not a mistake. How did God uniquely equip you for your task? What are the unique pros of your circumstances? Take a minute to look through the lists of ideas in "How Has God Equipped You for Your Task?" and "What Are the Pros of Your Circumstances?" Underline and highlight and be grateful.

Look hard with joy at the gifts you have, even the ones that might have been wrapped in pain or adversity. None of these are coincidences. Look at your life with a new set of eyes; God has uniquely prepared *you* to build this strong family.

How Has God Equipped You for Your Task?

- ☐ Do you love adventure? Can you make people smile with spontaneous humor?
- ☐ Do you feel things deeply? Can you detect minuscule changes in others' temperaments and know intuitively how each person is doing?
- ☐ Are you artistic? Can you make a space or a meal beautiful?
- ☐ Do you have a lot of energy? Can you survive on little sleep?
- ☐ Do you remember people's birthdays and give great gifts?
- ☐ Are you a take-charge personality? Is it easy for you to lead?
- ☐ Are you a peacemaker? Do you have a warm presence?
- ☐ Are you a great multitasker? Can you accomplish a lot in a short amount of time?
- ☐ Are you neat and tidy? Are you great at sensing when things need to be organized?
- ☐ Are you good at operations, making things run smoothly?
- ☐ Are you kind and thoughtful?
- ☐ Are you careful? Don't miss much?
- ☐ Are you organized?
- ☐ Are you playful?

What Are the Pros of Your Circumstances?

- ☐ Do you have a strong support system and community?
- ☐ Do you have grandparents, uncles, or aunts who love the snot out of your kids?
- ☐ Do you have financial breathing room?
- ☐ What is great about where you live?
- ☐ Did you grow up with strong examples of healthy families?
- ☐ Do you have a motherhood mentor you admire?
- ☐ Are you able to stay home with your kids? Wow. What a gift—time!
- ☐ Are you able to homeschool? Again—gift of time!
- ☐ Was your family of origin a hot mess? This can morph into its own uniquely powerful motivation. You know the importance of this calling. You know which mistakes you will not repeat.
- ☐ Have you overcome hardship and trauma? You are a model of strength and perseverance to your family—a true gift.

GETTING REAL ABOUT YOUR *WEAKNESSES*

But what about that elephant in the room . . . what about the hard things? Everyone has liabilities. When I was a sophomore in high school, my cousin/best friend called me a pious brat in a heated fight. I was utterly thunderstruck. Me? Pious? I was very lacking in self-awareness. A lack of self-awareness makes your liabilities even more so. We have to know what we are bad at.

That might be your problem, too, but more likely you know what you stink at. More likely, your failures or struggles are weighing you down subtly. What is the right thing to do with our hard things? I have two suggestions.

First, admit and pray. Bring your weakness out in the open. Example: *God, I acknowledge that I have massive anxiety. It often interferes with my ability to serve and love You and others. Will You help me deal with this? In Your mercy and strength, will You take this weakness and instead of letting it harm others, will You redeem it and use it for good? Amen.*

Then we do our best to fulfill our calling in the strength and wisdom He provides and leave the results to Him.

Second, have support systems in place. Do you have a plan in place to help you with your liability, or are you kind of ignoring it and hoping it goes away? Here are some concrete examples:

Example 1: Your extended family is complicated. Are you proactively inviting "substitute" support systems into your own life and the lives of your kids?

Example 2: You aren't naturally organized. Do you let your husband or another trusted person give you advice? Do you read books and listen to podcasts for tips?

Example 3: You're not a strong personality, and you have a strong-willed child. Are you letting your child steamroll you, or are you working hard to be a strong and loving parent?

What this inventory category *isn't* meant to do is to be a burden, an opportunity for self-loathing, and a piling on to your to-do list. Rather, the next time you feel overwhelmed by your own weaknesses as you seek to build a strong family, take comfort that there is a path forward: pray, lean on others, repeat.

One more word of encouragement. Don't let the enemy convince you that your Hard Things are too hard or too many. In the words of Paul David Tripp,

> *God never calls us to a task without giving us what we need to do it.* God never sends you into anything without going with you. . . . This is the story of the whole Bible. This is why God sent his Son to earth. . . .
>
> What does this have to do with parenting? Everything! It means that if you are God's child, it is impossible for you to be left to your own limited package of resources. . . . He knows how hard your task is. He knows that it drives you beyond the borders of your patience and wisdom. He knows that there are times when you feel that you have no clue of what you're doing. He knows there are moments when you wish you could quit and walk away. . . . He knew what every piece of your struggle would be as a parent, so he knew that the only thing that would help you would be himself.[5]

Some of the strongest families I know were forged while desperate mothers were on their knees daily, begging God for relief and guidance. Like I mentioned before, my Grammy, the matriarch of our amazing family, faced many of the hardest things you could think of—poverty, constant upheaval and moves, health issues, no outside support, a lonely marriage. Similarly, my mom is one of my heroes (what a family she has grown!), and her life has not been easy either. So many of the struggles she faced were unknown to us kids until years later. One thing we did know: while my dad was always a loving, faithful father, he was gone a lot with work. My mom's support system was nonexistent, aside from calls to her sisters while washing dishes, the phone cradled on her shoulder. I now know she also battled significant health issues and ongoing fatigue, even facing seasons of profound loneliness and depression. My mom is the best mom ever. *And* there were days she didn't think she could function. She would wake up and beg God for strength to love others. He showed up. He promises us that His strength is made perfect in our weakness.[6]

As you seek your strong family, *you do not have to be perfect.* Maybe your places of deep weakness are exactly where He will meet you.

SUMMING IT UP

- Before you can have the family you want, you have to get real about the family you have.
- You have limited capacity. Spend your time on the things that only you can do.
- Godly self-care helps you do your job better.
- You have unique gifts to raise a strong family.
- You have liabilities, too, but commit these to God; His strength is made perfect in our weakness.

TALKING IT OVER

1. What do you think is the biggest struggle you face in building a strong family?
2. Which things on your plate are things that only you can do, and which could someone else do?
3. How would you assess yourself in each of the four inventory areas? Color in the thermometers below to indicate your "temperature." Ask God to show you how you could move closer to thriving in each area.

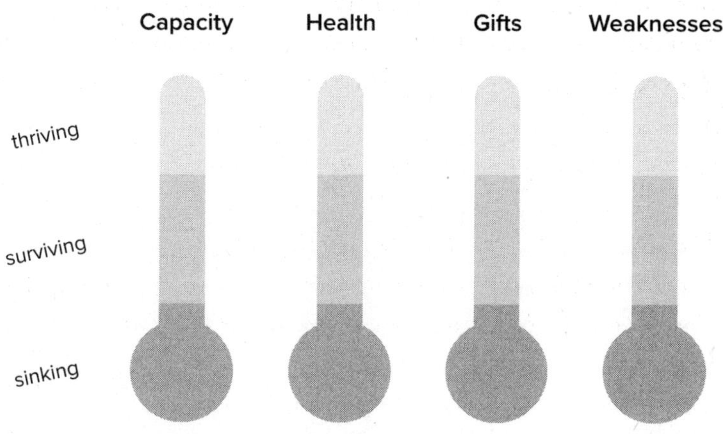

COMING HOME

1. If you haven't already, use the blank page at the end of this chapter to jot down all the things you do in life. Be simultaneously amazed and overwhelmed at all you do. Then, pray about off-loading some of the things you're doing solely out of obligation.
2. Ask your kids what you do best as a mom.
3. Think of one new self-care habit you could try out this season.

One Family's Story: The Lukes

Both Jim and Carrie grew up with challenges in their families of origin, and they have still built a beautiful family. I am so grateful to Carrie for sharing her story.

I was twenty-four when my daughter Maggie was born and had never really been around children. But when they put Maggie in my arms for the first time, I felt like I had come home to myself. She was very much wanted.

By God's grace I found myself in a parenting Bible study at church that taught me about boundaries with love. As our girls grew, we did our best to implement what I had learned.

Our daughters always enjoyed their room time, allowing me much-needed breaks. We read a ton, and our home was a home of stories. We kept a consistent dinnertime, and the girls and I read the Bible each morning at breakfast. We went to church consistently and invested in our church family. We limited screen time and sugar and video games. We played outside a lot. Even if they just took a blanket outside to read, we were outside for my own sanity.

When Mags turned four, the bottom fell out of my life, because that was the age I was when I was severely abused. I became depressed and sought help, but the wheels fell off of our lives. I was homeschooling and having terrible nightmares. This is where community was so important. I had friends who would watch the girls, no questions asked, so I could go to my counseling appointments.

As I healed and learned more about the truth of my own story, along with Jim doing the same, we put up boundaries with our families of origin, where there was no repentance from them. This has been costly, but in the end has saved us.

One important thing that was different than my upbringing was that I knew what it felt like to be blamed for your parents' problems. I refused to do that to my daughters. If I was having a hard day, I did not take it out on them. We just went to the park or the library or Chick-fil-A. If I needed to cry, I cried, but I told them it was not about them or our family. I gave them the words they needed to feel secure but allowed them their innocence.

When Mags began asking questions about sex, I prayed and I showed up in a way that was healthy for her. I did not talk about my abuse. I told her about God's design for procreation and pleasure. I wanted her to have her own experiences and not be burdened by my own.

When my girls became teenagers, I did not want them to feel the pain I had experienced. One night, I felt Jesus saying to me, "Carrie, I cannot get to Maggie because you are always there before Me. You need to give her some space, so that I have room to meet her in a real way." That was very powerful. I was still there for my daughters, but I didn't try to fix everything.

When they grew up and left home, the Holy Spirit began bringing to mind ways I had let my daughters down. Instead of rationalizing, I was able to go to my daughters and say that I was sorry. It is never too late to repent as long as it is sincere and genuine. I let them put words to their feelings. Now they are so good with things that they just say, "Mom. Enough. You did great."

2

PERSPECTIVE

On Digging Holes and Eating Pie

We cannot assume that children will know what our priorities are: we must live our priorities.

GORDON NEUFELD AND GABOR MATÉ
Hold On to Your Kids

The last time we were at a concert of our favorite singer, Andrew Peterson, he said, "Now I'm going to play you a song I wrote for my wife." That piqued my interest. He rarely mentions his wife in his songs, so I thought, *Wow! I can't wait to hear this. I wonder what sort of love song this will be.* I was a little bummed to realize the name of the song was "Planting Trees." *This is not a great start,* I thought. Is there anything more unsexy? Planting anything is the worst. It looks good in *Magnolia Journal*, but when you (and not Joanna Gaines) are the one out there getting ridiculously hot and sticky and dirty, trying to hack away at ground that is suddenly the density of a bowling ball, you realize what God meant when He told Adam the ground was cursed. Thanks, Adam.

Last summer my husband and I got in an argument about what size hole one should dig to plant a tomato seedling. Hot tip for wives: if your husband works in the landscaping business, he does not like it when you "ask him questions" about the size of the hole he dug. Tuck that one away. Apparently the size of a hole needed for a minuscule tomato plant is way bigger than you thought it needed to be. Even with that expert hole-digging, though, our tomato plants were a grave disappointment and the cucumbers so bitter that not even the chickens would eat them. This year we relied on the professionals and ordered from our local CSA farm market. Frankly, I have lost patience with gardening. You plant something, go to all that work, and *maybe* you get a good crop? Maybe you don't! You just have to wait and hope.

And then to plant a tree! My, you won't see the fruit of all that work for years! In fact, depending on your age, and the tree's age, and the weather and soil, and other Landscapery Things, it may actually be your kids, or your grandkids, or the people who buy your house later who finally get to eat good peach cobbler. You spend all this time and sweat and money to plant something that *you may never actually see the fruit of.* To be honest with you, I'm shocked there are so many trees in the world.

Back to Andrew Peterson's wife. The more I think about it, I wonder if instead of being disappointed that her husband wrote a song in her honor about digging holes and watching branches grow, perhaps she actually felt very *seen*.

Building a strong family, as Andrew's wife has evidently learned, involves hard, painful, sweaty labor, all the while with the understanding that you might not be enjoying shade in that corner of the yard for a decade or more. What hope! What perspective! The reason I'm bad at gardening is the same reason I struggle with parenting: it is not natural for me to take the long view.

But taking the long view is essential for strong-family growing. I've thought about it, and I think this long-view (eternal, even) perspective primarily impacts two aspects of being a wife and mom: your time and your decision-making.

TAKING THE LONG VIEW IMPACTS YOUR *TIME*

Growing a strong family involves dumping your time into activities that often, like gardening, aren't fun, don't give you immediate satisfaction but, you hope, might grow into something really, really beautiful. There are so many of these small tasks inherent in every day of being a good mother. I know you are already giving your time to these little things. Keep going. Don't give up.

One opportunity I have every day to lay down my time is through our "Morning Time." This is a part of our homeschooling routine. Each day, we read from a devotional, a history book, a science book, and a novel. In the circles of Really Wise Homeschooling Mothers, it is an accepted fact that Morning Time is about the best thing you can do in your homeschool. The thing you will look back on and love more than anything. I am taking Cindy Rollins at her word on this,[1] because every. single. day. I do not want to do morning time. I am never in the mood to do morning time. It feels like a waste. It is so long—an hour or more of my life when at least a hundred tasks are calling me. Where I sit, I have a direct view of the kitchen island, which is undoubtedly scattered with Things I Want to Clean Up. Then there are emails, appointments, things to order, texts to write. I have to try really hard to ignore the noise of those beckoning tasks and "waste" an hour reading about Galileo, butterflies, and so on. This is an act of faith. I am believing that in twenty years, *Little Women* is going to mean something in my children's lives.

Even if you are not a homeschooling mom, I am sure that you can relate to my frustration in some way. We *want* to invest in our families, but we have so many temptations and distractions. One book that encouraged me in this area is Rebekah Merkle's *Eve in Exile*. This book made me clean bathrooms much more frequently, with more joy, than I did before. That is a powerful book, is it not? The author doesn't speak of bathrooms per se, but of the joy that comes to a woman investing her time in her homemaking. The book prompted me to think, *What could it look like to lavish my family with my gifts and time?* Not to give them the leftovers, but the firstfruits?

Many of us moms give the leftovers to our family. I am guilty of this. It feels more important to be the chair of a committee and organize a Great Thing for our city or church or Internet Followers. It feels less than strategic, honestly. Why would I pour into just a few, when I could serve many? Merkle asserts that we are most alive and most ourselves when we dump out our lives to fill, subdue, and help in our sphere of home.

Does this mean that if we are moms, we should only stay at home and never do anything outside of the home? No! Not at all! Merkle says that *it's not about where you are; it's about where you are pointed.*[2] In a related book, *Simplified Organization*, Mystie Winckler says that when we pour out our gifts and our time for our families, it makes us *more* energized and equipped to serve the rest of the world, not less.[3] I have certainly found this to be true in my own life. Thriving in the home overflows into everything else. When my family gets my first and best, the rest of life feels hopeful and more organized. I have an abundance of creativity. I get bandwidth to love the world. As un-fun as it feels in the moment, I don't often regret the time I've invested in my home or family. I've never regretted spending an afternoon organizing a closet so that it better serves my family's needs. I don't look back and think, *I wish I hadn't made that meal special.* I don't regret one date night or vacation. I've stopped and started a lot of chore and behavior systems in my day, but I don't regret trying.

Is this something that you've found to be true? When you think of investing your time in your family, what is most life-giving to you? I know that each of us mamas represent a unique story, with our own schedules, family dynamics, callings, and passions. Isn't it exciting that it can look so different for all of us? Think back to the Honesty chapter and all your many gifts! God knows us, knows our talents, and knows what our families need. What could this look like for you?

TAKING THE LONG VIEW IMPACTS YOUR *CHOICES*

Taking the long view greatly impacts how we make decisions. My goodness, isn't parenting chock-full of options? I was shocked to learn that the average person makes about thirty-five thousand decisions in a day.[4] Do you think it is more for mothers? I do. I have found that the older my kids get, the weightier and more overwhelming my decisions are, which explains why deciding what to make for dinner often threatens to undo me completely. Dinnertime decisions aside, the stakes keep getting higher.

Someone who has her eye fixed on the fruit ten years down the road makes different decisions than someone who simply wants today to be easy. As I write this, my son is fifteen and still without a phone. This is getting hard. Whatever decisions we make about technology over the next few years, we are trying really hard to keep our eye on the trees we are planting. We are trying to grow character, strong family ties, self-control, courage, and purity. This means our lives right now might be more annoying and less convenient than they could be if we would just buy him an iPhone. I don't personally mind the inconvenience of my kid not having a smartphone, but it's hard to think about him feeling embarrassed in front of his friends. But then again! We have the long view. We are digging holes for the fruit we want later.

On a quite different level, my nine-year-old daughter asked me last night to play a game with her. I did not want to play a game. I was overstimulated and had dishes to wash. Long-term perspective is really the only rational reason an exhausted someone would play

Chicken Dominoes ("Cluck, Cluck!") at 8:37 p.m. with dishes in the sink.

Here's another one. Years ago, I ran into a friend at Target. I had just had my third child, and I told her things were going pretty well. "Wait until those two start fighting," she said with a scoff and a glance at my middle and youngest children. Darn that prophecy. When they play together, it's the sweetest thing, but as the Southern moms like to say, "They have their moments." Because I take the long view, disciplining their "moments" has a different hue than it otherwise would. If I only cared about today, I would simply shut them in their rooms when they are arguing about whose elbow was in the middle of the table first. (If I could use emojis, it would be the eye roll here.) Instead of just shutting them up to make them stop being so annoying, a long-view approach could be to bring the Most Guilty Party into my room to sit with me on the gray upholstered chairs. I would use square breathing exercises to make it through his or her unnecessarily long play-by-play of The Alleged Elbow Incident, and then I'd ask something like this: "Do you want your kids to have cousins to play with like you do? Okay, great. You do. Well, that means you have to be friends with your sister. How can you be a better friend?" It's probably a needless interjection that rarely does someone say, "Wow, Mom, that is such a good point. Here's how I want to be a better friend." Nope—it is usually a long and painful exercise for everyone involved. But when I have the long view, with my vision fixed on the goal of a strong, healthy family, the painful exercise can be endured. Keep thinking about that peach pie when you're digging the holes.

This perspective issue will impact so many of the chapters to come, because so many of them involve making hard choices. Perspective is the Gatorade that powers you through the workout. Making memories? Annoying, lots of work, but so worth it! Look what we're building! Forgiving people and offering grace? Ugh, is anything more unnatural than that? But look at that end goal! Worth the discomfort and then some!

I have been thinking about that phrase "You reap what you sow." It's such a common phrase that we gloss over without unpacking. But let's do that. (Brace yourself—more landscaping talk.) Imagine you go to a nursery and bring home an apple tree. You bring the plant home, dig your hole, and nestle it in the earth. You wait, and eventually little apple blossoms appear on your tree! Now, your crop may or may not be great, but the one thing that is sure is that you would never see cucumbers where you planted apples. That would be insane. It is not what happens in the world. What you plant in the ground is what will grow.

This is not merely an agricultural observation. This is a true, biblical description of how life works.[5] What you plant in your life is generally what you end up with. If I spend my time exercising, I will reap a body that is fit. If I spend time investing in a social calendar, I will end up with memories and connections to the people I have invested in. If I spend time memorizing Bible verses, I will end up with Scripture in my head to guide me through my daily decisions. If I spend my years and skills in a sales job, I will end up with money and corporate expertise. If I spend time scrolling Instagram, I will reap . . . well, I am not exactly sure what I would reap there. That is a little unsettling to think about.

Do we want to reap the kind of family who wants to come home? Do we want to reap friendships with our adult kids? Do we want to reap the kind of family who loves vacationing together and all the aunts and uncles and cousins enjoy deep, real bonds and don't just merely "get along" for a week? Do we want to lay our heads on the pillow every night and feel the unmatched joy of knowing that our children are walking in the truth?[6]

I don't mean to imply that this is some kind of guaranteed

parenting formula or a vending machine situation. You can't press the right buttons and expect what you want to pop out. Unfortunately there are no guarantees of all those wonderful things I listed. But just like there are no guarantees you will end up with apples, you certainly won't have any at all if you don't plant the trees. Planting seeds is the best chance you have. It is a truth almost beautiful enough to motivate me to plant literal trees. Almost.

SUMMING IT UP

- It's essential to keep the long view when you're building a strong family, because it is exhausting work that doesn't always reward in the moment.
- When we pour out our time for our homes and families, it makes us *more* equipped to serve the world, not less.

TALKING IT OVER

1. Think of a gift or skill you have. How could you use that gift to bless your family this week?
2. What's something you do with your time that you won't see the payoff for now, but you're trusting will pay off later?
3. Go back over those lists of gifts that you have from chapter 1. What would it look like to fully, joyfully invest them in your family? Could you do it for a month and see what happens?

COMING HOME

1. Play a board game with your family today.
2. If you have older kids, take a minute and compliment them for an area in which they're demonstrating maturity.
3. Using your unique gifts, think of a way to make one family dinner this week a little more special—decor, dessert, fun conversation topics?

One Family's Story: The Wrays

I have known the Wrays for over twenty years. Their kids went to college with Todd and me and remain good friends of ours. Their giant family is FUN! And we also deeply respect them.

When Bruce and I got married, we were blessed to have some helpful things passed down from the previous generation: the importance of marriage, the family unit, and the extended family; the importance of deep and enduring friendships; a strong work ethic; a sense of community involvement; and hospitality. We also shared some unhealthy legacies: emotionally distant fathers, lack of prayer and Bible study in the home, and excessive drinking.

When I look back, there are a few things I wish we had done differently. I wish we had sought out mentors. We didn't know to do that. We were mostly flying blind and could have benefited greatly from others' experience. Looking back, if I could have chosen mentors, I would choose the people our kids have become! They are fulfilling God's assignment to parent their kids so much better than we ever did. I am super thankful for that!

I also feel we were in survival mode too much. We weren't intentional regarding faith and goals until the kids were older, at which time we finally realized there would be great value in prioritizing well. I would have loved if we could have done more prayer journals and family outreach. I wish we had spent more time with the kids, specifically reading to them. Some things I'm glad we did:

- Having family breakfast for thirty minutes every morning once the older kids started missing dinners due to jobs and sports
- Having a required family time on Sunday afternoons

- Starting a little family business while they were young, so they learned about working together and finding their best spot in the venture
- Individual weekend retreats so Bruce and I could regroup and reprioritize; one of us would go and the other stayed home with the kids
- House swaps with other young parents for an occasional break without the expense
- Opening our home often to host Bible study groups, Young Life, and lots of parties!
- Limiting TV and movies and devices

Take the time to know each child, helping them find their passion, abilities, gifts, and interests. You will both be so blessed.

3

AUTHORITY

Leading Your Little Pack with Love

Establishing authority early in little things is doing gospel work.

PAUL DAVID TRIPP, *Parenting*

I would give two pieces of advice to new moms. The first piece is this. Take a photo every day and print your photo book every year. If you don't follow this advice, it is very possible that your oldest child will be almost sixteen, and you will be like thirteen years behind in photo albums. It's not like I know this from personal experience, but a girl I know had that happen. *Ahem.*

The second piece of advice is this. For the first six months of being a new mom, just survive. If you just survive, you are doing absolutely fantastic at life and deserve an A-plus. Go, you! My friend told me when my child was in the newborn stage that I needed to change my voicemail message to say, "Hi. This is Jessica. I just had a baby. I will call you back in three years." There is some profound wisdom in this.

There is, however, a part B to this second piece of advice. After the first six months, you will start to find your wings again. You will find yourself having the capacity to do things like: Shower. Clean a toilet. Paint your toenails, even. It will feel absolutely invigorating. When this Second Wind appears, you need to begin wrapping your head around a very important concept of motherhood, and that is this: YOU ARE THE BOSS.

There are three possible reasons that this role is very difficult to accept. The first is that, at the beginning, babies are beautiful, helpless little marvels of wonderfulness. They're yummy and harmless. But there comes this moment (it totally varies at what month) when you will, unbelievably, catch a whiff of something that almost seems like . . . disobedience? It's incomprehensible. *Surely that child did not just throw that sippy cup down for the fifth time with a vengeful look in my direction. My precious little angel?! It cannot be.*

But it was.

And then it happens again, and it's undeniable. Alas, this precious child is somehow not perfect. So that's sad. And you are never quite ready for it.

The second reason it is difficult to accept that you are in charge is that you as a mother may, actually, not prefer to be A Person Who Is in Charge. Some of us bossy firstborns (**clears throat**) have lived for this moment and step quite readily into the role of Commander in Chief. So that helps. But others of us—more naturally likable and pleasant—prefer a more supporting role in life. These are helpers, tender hearts, playmates. It is not super fun for these people to have to suddenly be in charge.

The third reason it's difficult to accept that you are the boss is that the child may turn out to be a person who would actually prefer to be in charge! Never mind the age difference . . . they want you to give them the reins and let them steer. So when reasons #2 and #3 combine, that makes for a rather amusing scenario in the checkout line at Target if there are orange Tic Tacs at eye level.

Though amusing, it is still painful to watch. I can spot a mismatch like this within about seven seconds.

Are you destined for public tantrums and internal strife if you don't relish being the boss as a mother? Of course not! The word I am getting at with all this talk about who's in charge is *authority*. What exactly do I mean by this word? And why is authority getting one whole chapter in the book? This is not random. Loving authority is the "salt" of the family soup. You really can't make anything good without it.

WHY WE NEED LOVING AUTHORITY

The best way I can define what healthy authority looks like is to talk about a show Todd and I used to watch. Back when we had no dollars, our primary entertainment was waiting for Netflix DVDs to arrive in the mailbox and then savoring one episode per evening. Sometimes someone would forget to put the old DVD in the mailbox, and this added extra days to the wait. That was a heavy load for the responsible party to bear. We watched these episodes on a mini DVD player that we set on Todd's legs until I got worried it was killing all his sperm and we bought a real TV like a bunch of rich people.

One show we loved featured a dog trainer who helped people with dogs that were out of control. Some of the dogs were vicious beasts who bit and drew blood, and others did weird things like bark for three hours if someone sat on their favorite pink pillow.

This show was such a study in personality. Human personality, that is! You eventually realized that when the trainer came in to save the dog owners from "bad" dogs, *he was training the owner more than the dog*. He emphasized the importance of dog owners channeling a calm and firm demeanor. I can't tell you how often this idea pops into my psyche and guides me in an hour of parental confusion.

Now, don't get me wrong. I know our children are not dogs. As beings made in the image of their Creator, they are clearly much more complex and worthy of all the dignity that comes with that. But bear with me. See if you notice any similarities to parenting here that might give us insights into our challenging task. For one thing, dogs need to have a "pack leader." The problem arises when dog owners do not know how to be the pack leader, to be the one in authority. If domestic dogs don't have a pack leader, one of them will step up to be the leader but may do so anxiously. Sometimes in the show, the owners were *trying* to be in charge, but they didn't really know how to go about it.

Good authority—for dogs or children or anyone else—is not yelling to get someone to obey in a language they don't understand. It is not anxiously *hoping* someone will obey. It is not asking quietly and seeing what will happen. And it is not attempting to control every little thing. It is paying attention. It is fearlessly putting boundaries in place and standing firm on them. It is knowing—deep down—that you are in charge. And then being calm and happy and going about your unrelated business.

Did you pick up the interesting parallels there?

At the end of each show, when the trainer had rehabilitated the dog (slash owner), everyone was so much happier. The owners could do things like sit on the pink pillows and have people over for dinner without them getting eaten by angry Chihuahuas. You know—live ordinary lives.

The newly happy dog owners were relieved. The dogs were relieved. It was life, functioning as it was meant to be.

Here it is, bluntly: dogs and children need leaders who are ready to be leaders. Neither dogs nor children ostensibly appear to want this, and sometimes they fight it. But deep down, they really, really do want this.

God designed life to be this way.[1] We were made to be subject to the appropriate authorities. If we try to live against the way we were made, things go south. It would be like making mashed potatoes with a garlic press. You can try it, but it would be frustrating and messy and take forever, because the garlic press is not being used in the way that it was created for.

Let me put this another way. If you don't teach your kids to obey you, you aren't loving them well, and they won't reach their potential. Their life will be harder and messier. And most notably here, building that strong family will be one hundred times more difficult because you will be swimming upstream, alone. When you exert loving authority, when you teach your kids to submit their little wills to a leader who can be trusted, you are giving them an incredible gift. I believe that so many of the problems facing younger generations stem from the fact that kids are being left to write their own rules.

Particularly for our purposes of building a strong family, authority is most certainly needed. In coming chapters we'll look at the characteristics of a strong family, like quality time, friendship, connection, loyalty. All of these require someone to lead the pack. You can't really make the magic of a strong family if some of these characteristics are optional for your children.

WHAT LOVING AUTHORITY LOOKS LIKE

At the same time, you can't build a wonderful, happy family if you're a cruel drill sergeant. I have many friends who grew up in that type of love-bare home, and no matter how many vacations their families took together, the kids felt empty. Authority is a really un-fun-sounding word, but this space we are going for—this "loving authority"—is really the absolute gold of parenting. It can wear many different names. I once came across a description of "elephant parenting" (in contrast to the classic "helicopter mom" or über-strict "tiger parents").[2] "Elephant parents" are intuitive, gentle, loving, and strong. It is commonly thought of as the healthiest style of parenting. I actually considered writing a book called *Elephant Moms* for a second, and then my agent said that mothers may not respond favorably to being likened to elephants. Probably a good call.

Similarly, psychologist Diana Baumrind published parenting studies over the last forty years. She separated parenting styles into three types, which can be thought of as "too hard," "too soft," and "just right." Kind of like Goldilocks. Here's the "just right" description: "'Just Right' parents communicate their love for their child, but they also enforce rules fairly and consistently. The rules may bend on occasion, when necessary, but they don't break. . . . 'Just Right' parents are strict, within reasonable bounds, and also loving."[3]

I think my parents excelled at this style.

When I was nineteen, my parents got a little gray Volvo for my sister and me to drive back and forth to college, through the winding (often snowy) roads from North Carolina to Grove City, Pennsylvania. It wasn't a new vehicle, but I loved that little car. The thing about Volvos is that they are deemed very safe, but there was only one dealership in our area where you could have them repaired. Ironically, getting in and out of the dealership involved a super-dangerous U-turn crossing of three lanes of traffic. As I was the kind of teen driver who had asked, "Which is the brake, and which is the gas?" on my first day of driver's ed, I would not say I excelled in situations requiring this sort of automotive finesse. The first time I encountered this scary intersection, my dad was driving his car in front of me, and I was right behind in the little gray Volvo.

As we approached the intersection, I felt my anxiety rising. But my dad stopped, rolled down his window, and held up one finger, meaning I was to wait. As the cars blew by, I calmed down, realizing that he was going to ensure our two cars could cross at the same time. My breathing slowed as I fixed my eyes on his finger. Finally, he beckoned. "Come on," his hand said, with a little bit of urgency. "It's safe now." He went first; I followed, not a doubt in the world that I and my little gray Volvo would be perfectly fine.

Isn't it funny how certain incidents stay so poignant and fresh in your mind? What a weird memory. We drove across a road. And yet, twenty years later it still evokes a deep feeling in me.

I share that story because I think it's a bit of a picture of this loving authority: "I am not entirely in control, but I am safe. I am in someone's care." My parents did not parent perfectly, but we always knew someone was at the helm. Someone was always home, both physically and metaphorically. Someone was paying attention.

My parents did not slather the home with a layer of restrictive regulations. I would not have said they were strict parents. I honestly remember very few times I was ever punished. They kept us close and redirected in subtle ways.

WHEN YOU FACE RESISTANCE

Once you have established your authority, you don't have to flaunt it at every juncture. It is a fact. Have you settled in your head that you are the loving authority? Are you good with this role?

Some of the principles and ideas in this book are going to be amazing and fun for your kids. You'll be reminded to give more hugs, pay for their sibling dates, go on adventures, listen better, see things from their perspective, and more. But some of the ideas may not be a welcome change for all the members of your household. Some may balk, resist.

What then?

You have to be able to muster the internal energy to do the right thing anyway. To do so, you will first need to cement your belief about who's in charge, then carefully choose your battles, and, when you need further support, invoke higher authorities. Here's how this works.

Cement Your Belief About Who's in Charge

Above all else, you must be convinced that loving, kind authority is best for your kids. Sometimes when we don't enforce things, it's because we aren't sure it's worth the pushback we will get.

And maybe it's not for you.

You get to decide. Just like I said in the introduction, you are steering the ship on this journey. You get to make your own choices about parenting. Don't do it because I said so. Maybe you need to spend a minute reflecting or journaling to figure out if you agree with me. If you need some help sorting this out, see the "Is Loving Authority Worth It for You?" exercise.

One thing that helps me when I'm feeling uneasy about imparting necessary discipline is to remember that loving discipline is actually a kindness to the child. Even though it feels super unfun for everyone in the moment, it is ultimately not doing them any favors if we ignore behavior that's disagreeable or unpleasant. Psychologist Jordan B. Peterson says, "You love your kids, after all. If their actions make you dislike them, think what an effect they will have on other people, who care much less about them than you."[4] This may seem like a blunt way to put it, but it helps me remember that discipline, done well, is ultimately helpful to our kids in their relationships both inside and out of the home.

In addition to the social incentive, I appreciate the spiritual rationale to discipline in *Parenting* by Paul David Tripp. He says, "Capitalize on the little moments God will give you when your children are still young. . . . Don't tell yourself that those little moments of resistance to your authority (what to eat, what to wear, when to go to bed, what to watch, doing chores, etc.) are unimportant because the issue at hand is not that important. . . .

Is Loving Authority Worth It for You?

1. Think about other kids you know. Who are your favorite kids to be around? Why?
2. Would your kids' lives be easier or harder if they could accept a "no" answer nicely?
3. Would your life be easier or harder if your kids could accept a "no" answer nicely?
4. When you picture the ideal mother, what does she do when her kids argue with her?
5. If you are married, what does your husband think about this?
6. The next time your kid is kind of being naughty, pretend that it was a random kid in your neighborhood behaving this way. How would you think his or her parents should respond?
7. What are you most afraid will happen if you are the "pack leader" for your kids?
8. If you had clearly stated consequences in place and a plan for following through on them, would it be easier to stick to your guns?

Be thankful for these little moments. Don't look at them as the bad moments of parenting, as hassles and interruptions; these are the good moments of parenting."[5]

Choose Your Battles

I'm sure you can think of plenty of areas right now where you have prime opportunities for applying discipline. Maybe it's the kid who refuses to stay buckled in the van, or the one who comes out thirty-six times after bedtime. It could be the one who sneaks the iPad away, or who argues every time you tell them to put on pajamas, or who refuses to do homework without a giant emotional production. I mentioned earlier that effective authority is not trying to control every little thing our dogs—or children—do. This is confusing to dogs. And children. While there are, truly, ten thousand things we want our kids to do, we have to be selective.

If this is an area you struggle with, pick a thing or two that needs to be picked. Then stand your ground. This means you choose a consequence and enforce it with cheerful indifference. Be firm, be pleasant, be kind. Jordan B. Peterson quips, "First: limit the rules. . . . Second: use the least force necessary to enforce those rules."[6]

The interesting thing about this approach is that compliance has a pleasant ripple effect. Even when you pick one little battle, your kids will be comforted by the fact that you are truly holding the reins, and a lot of the other battlegrounds will disappear or become smaller. Don't try to address everything at once. Pick one thing. Meet with the child. Let them know in the kindest, smilingest, calmest way possible that their former habits will no longer be happening. With my kids, I say it as if it is already true: "We don't do this in our house anymore."

The first time is the worst. Also unpleasant are the next eighty-seven times. But eventually, as my mom would tell me, "You will win this, Jessie. You are the boss here." And don't forget: we hold the keys to the car, the remote to the Switch, and the credit card that buys the fruit snacks. That's pretty powerful leverage.

I think this idea of choosing our battles is especially important to keep at the forefront of our minds as we navigate technology decisions with our kids. I bet as you consider choosing your battles you will land on tech choices as the battles worth choosing. Listen to your gut. If you have a hunch that something isn't healthy for your child or your family, don't ignore it. God gave you razor-sharp parenting instincts just for this reason. As He nudges you, go with confidence that you are making the right choices, even if you don't win any popularity contests at the time.

Invoke the Higher Authorities

When it's time to make a tough parenting call, I know how defeating and lonely it can feel. It's no fun being "the bad guy." But remember that you are not alone. We truly have been given a job from God to raise kids who learn to obey us and obey Him. If they can't submit to our authority, they will have much more difficulty submitting to God. Again, it's worth noting Paul David Tripp's wisdom on this topic: "What God has called you to is to daily confront your children with how beautiful, helpful, and patient God's authority is. You want to be used of God to help your children to begin to believe that submission to authority is where life and freedom are to be found."[7]

When I'm navigating the nitty-gritty of a hard discipline issue with one of my children, I have found it helpful to say, "Listen. I know I am not a perfect mom. But I'm really trying to do my job right. God gave me the job of raising you to love and follow Him, and I am trying to do the job He gave me to do."

SUMMING IT UP

- Loving authority is essential.
- Kids long for loving authority.
- Spiritually speaking, the goal of loving authority is that as our children learn to trust and obey us, they also learn to trust and obey their heavenly Father.

TALKING IT OVER

1. What kind of authority was modeled in your families of origin?
2. When you picture the ideal mother, what does she do when her kids argue with her?

3. Do you feel like you model a calm and firm demeanor? What would it look like if you did?

COMING HOME

1. Play Simon Says or Red Light Green Light with your kids—fun ways to get them in the habit of listening to your instructions!
2. Say "yes" to one thing and "no" to one thing your kids ask you for today. Which is easier?

4

PARTNERSHIP

Leaning on Help for the Journey

There's a place where you run when you are hiding.
Would you take me with you when you go?

ANDREW OSENGA, "I'm on Your Side"

Recently my brother-in-law Grayson asked Todd and me when we knew we were going to marry each other. Todd quickly said, "Before we were dating." But for me, this was a complicated question. I would say I was not completely sure until we were walking back down the aisle, having said, "I do." This is not so much a statement about the fragility of our relationship as it is the fragility of, say, me as a person. I was a bit of a mess. But in my defense, when you have been through a broken engagement to someone else you had genuinely hoped to marry, it does tend to unsettle your confidence in picking a mate just a smidge. Hence, I kept thinking I must be making a mistake.

This made premarital counseling a bit more "exciting" than perhaps your typical round. Our pastor, Chip, was gifted in counseling, and I hung on his every gospel-centered word. He had us pegged. No one, perhaps, has captured our marriage in a nutshell better than this: "If your house catches on fire, Jessica will leap, screaming, into action with her ten-step plan, and Todd will be sitting comfortably in a chair waiting to see if the house really *is* on fire." As you might imagine, this dynamic creates an "exciting" tension from time to time.

Another thing our pastor shared that I have never forgotten is a quotation from Tim Keller: "If your marriage is strong, even if all the circumstances in your life around you are filled with trouble and weakness, it won't matter. You will be able to move out into the world in strength."[1] I have very much found this to be true. Todd and I don't fight much, but when we have an unresolved issue, it is like I am walking through the day in a terrible haze. Everything feels off. Even Todd, who is A Compartmentalizing Master, confesses that he feels unsettled and troubled when things aren't good between us.

The last fight Todd and I had occurred while we were visiting his parents over Christmas, so we had to walk around and pretend like everything was wonderful. That's really fun. Instead of joining the family on an outing to the park, I went to Target and ended up buying new underwear. It was fine, and honestly, I really needed new underwear, but this proves my point that you aren't your best Memory-Making Self when your marriage doesn't feel strong. Parenting is hard enough. Having a good partner can help propel you through the hard times.

Let me interject something here, before I go any further. *In case you are a single mom reading this right now, I hope you aren't beginning to feel like there is nothing in this chapter for you.* Similarly, if you are married and find yourself in a difficult season with your spouse, seeing a whole chapter devoted to partnership may cause you dread and pain. I see you. There are different types of partnership besides marriage. If you are a single mom, it will be even more important to find those supportive relationships. (Make sure you don't miss the end of this chapter!)

BUILDING A STRONG MARRIAGE

Herbert Lingren coauthored an eight-volume report on a ten-year study of family strengths. So this dude knows what he is talking about. He notes, "In intact families, the quality of the marriage was very important and a critical family resource. . . . *If the marriage was good, no matter what stressors occurred (from daily hassles to major accidents), the families that had a good marriage seemed to survive and do well.*"[2]

Similarly, an extensive 2002 report by the YMCA states that "the parents we interviewed who experience an excellent partner relationship . . . are more likely to feel successful and up to the challenges of parenting."[3]

I saw this in my own research as well. When I asked my email subscribers, "What is the biggest challenge you're facing right now?" a common thread throughout responses was lack of alignment in marriage affecting the family. Despite the many challenges inherent in parenting, many of the core issues involved the marriage partnership. "My husband and I disagree about the kids' education." "We differ in how we want to handle my son's misbehavior." "My husband works a lot, and I struggle to not feel resentful." "We have such different personalities. I wish he was more involved in family activities." And so on.

For those of us who are married, how do we strengthen our partnership and thus go forward with our best selves? Particularly, how do we do this throughout the various stages of parenting? In a darkly ironic twist, the times when you both most need a strong union are often the busiest and most difficult times to connect as a couple. How do you keep your marriage spark alive when you have LEGOs in your bed and/or teenagers awake later than you are?

Since the marriage partnership can have such a foundational impact on the health and strength of a family, it is worth taking time to reflect on how to keep it strong. To be honest, I have avoided this chapter a bit. I am not a marriage expert. I once threw my car keys across the room at my husband in an emotional outrage. Someone like that should probably not write publicly about marriage. And everyone's marriage is so different! How can I cover every situation?

Since marriage can be so integral in building a strong family, I'm going to share a few principles that I have learned over the years through my own experience and from the experience of Those Who Have Gone Before Me.

1. You don't have to have a strong marriage to have a strong family.

So maybe this sounds contradictory to the whole thing, but it is very, very true. Earlier I shared about my Grammy and the legacy of strong family she built. Grammy did not have a life-giving marriage. My Poppy was a fun-loving man, and I have wonderful memories of him, but from all appearances he was not the best husband. He was a dreamer and job-hopper; he moved their family thirty-four times as he chased horse-racing opportunities, most of which brought in little money.

When I was engaged to fiancé #1, my Grammy wrote me a letter. She had never, ever written a letter to me before. She shared her concerns about my fiancé, one of which was that he wouldn't be able to financially provide for me. I argued fiercely with her, both in my head and eventually in my own letter. When I told my mom about this, she cried. "I think that Grammy was thinking of her own marriage," my mom reflected.

My Grammy did not parent from a position of strength. She "moved out into the world," as Tim Keller put it, crippled by a painful marriage. And yet she built a legacy. How did she do it? *She clung to Jesus.* While a strong marriage is worth fighting for and is a balm and gift, it is not essential for building a close-knit family. In her weakness, Grammy hung on to Christ. He was her everything. Her life was very hard, much harder than it needed to be, but God worked anyway. And abundantly! God does that.

2. It is God who gives us the strength to love in marriage.

Birth control was a sort of poison to me. This is going to seem unrelated, but stick with me here. It literally made my hormones go berserk. I am hoping my editor lets me keep this in here because actually I don't think I am alone in this. I had such wild mood swings that in our first year of marriage (in which I threw the aforementioned car keys at my husband), I thought it would truly be a miracle if our marriage survived. We seemed so different. Today, our marriage is a source of strength and rich joy to me in a way that I would never have thought possible. This was a direct answer to prayer. If things seem dark and hard in your marriage, *pray*. I remember one epic fight in that awful first year. I left and drove to a nearby soccer field, where I wept in my car and begged God to show up and save our marriage. As He is so kind to do, He answered. Over and over again. (It started with me getting off birth control. Ha.) Anything good in our marriage is because He has given Todd and me the strength to love one another. In a funny, ironic twist, this often looks, for me, like taking a chill pill and, for Todd, like taking a don't-be-so-chill pill. So again. When your marriage feels desperate, look to our miracle-working God.

3. Don't let contempt take root in your marriage.

Psychologist John Gottman conducted four decades of research on marriage and concluded that the number one predictor of divorce is *contempt* in a marriage. What is contempt?

> When we communicate in this state, we are truly mean—we treat others with disrespect, mock them with sarcasm, ridicule, call them names, and mimic or use body language such as eye-rolling or scoffing. The target of contempt is made to feel despised and worthless.
>
> Contempt goes far beyond criticism. While criticism attacks your partner's character, contempt assumes a position of moral superiority over them.[4]

I remember hearing about the danger of contempt early on in our marriage, and I have developed a healthy fear of it in myself. As a person who can struggle with being sarcastic or critical, I have to fight to keep these feelings from taking permanent root in our relationship. As a parent, it is vitally important to present respect to your spouse publicly, because your kids are taking your cues. If you don't show respect to your spouse, they likely won't either. I try to be mindful of speaking respectfully of my husband to the kids, even if there is "more to the story." And when I fail and publicly disrespect him, I try to publicly apologize.

4. Fight daily to have a good marriage.

"Fight" feels like a dramatic word and makes me think of those late nights where you stay up and sort the thing out. That is part of it. But it's not just big moments like that; it is perhaps more frequently made up of smaller decisions here and there over time. It is so easy to coexist. What does it look like to fight for your marriage daily? I think my husband would say: Smiling when he comes home. Answering the phone cheerfully when he calls. Responding to his texts so he doesn't wonder if I'm dead. Not doubting whether he loves me. Being happy with my role in life. Doing my hair. Taking a shower after I have worked out. Noticing the ways he has loved me (acts of service—why do people never marry someone with the same love language??). Investing in our home and our family. Thanking him. Have you ever asked your husband how you can love him best? One friend of mine was shocked when her husband said, "I love your nails painted" (?!).

5. *Have fun in your marriage.*

Sometimes it seems like a wonder that at one time, so much of our relationship was fun and games, because currently it seems so little of it is. This is a shame. I could be wrong, but I think this Having Fun While Married element is slightly more important to most husbands than to wives. I tend to skip this one because it truly seems decadent and superfluous. It seems too good to be true. Date nights, getaways, shared hobbies, curling up and watching a show together, grabbing a glass of wine together at night, shutting the door and taking two minutes to catch up WITHOUT KIDS LISTENING—these feel like absolute luxuries that I have to earn by my good works and hard work. It is absolute good news that maybe this is precisely what I *should* be doing! In fact, this might be the most hopeful and delightful thing you read all day: go have a good time with your husband!

My aunt and uncle always seemed to do a good job of keeping their marriage strong. I asked my aunt for her secret and she said, "We forced ourselves to take date nights (and sometimes I didn't really want to!)." That was weirdly reassuring. I remember speaking with my neighbor Page one time (in the driveway, like you do). Page had three very young kids and was preparing to go away with her husband for a few nights. She said, "It always feels completely crazy right before we're leaving, but I think this is exactly what we should be doing. What is more important than building our marriage?" I honestly debated her in my head. *Isn't parenting important? Isn't staying on your budget important?* But now I think she was on to something.

Each stage of marriage has its own challenges. When you have very little children, you're physically exhausted, but they do, eventually, go to bed, and then you can have that time together. As they become teenagers, they start staying up late. So late. And they want to eat a second dinner, and a third dinner, and watch a show with you, and talk to you, and all their activities keep you running . . . This is a different sort of challenge for marriage!

This spring was completely nuts for our family. There were two or three weeks where it felt like my husband and I could hardly finish a conversation. In the midst of this, our generous neighbors offered to let us stay in their mountain cabin, which gave us something to look forward to. We plodded to the finish of that crazy season, telling ourselves that shortly, finally, we would be alone. In the mountains. We could make it! Just having a getaway on the calendar breathes its own sort of Life into your marriage. I got really, really mad at Todd the week before the trip, but I told myself, "Well, we can't get divorced. We have that amazing trip coming up." (That's a joke, in case you aren't sure.) But truly, we left those few, life-giving days thoroughly reenergized and with some takeaways:

- A getaway has to be at least two nights to be restful, but three or more is ideal.
- We actually do love being together.
- Not having to make your own food or DO ANYTHING is one of life's greatest gifts.
- Nature heals.
- We need to have a getaway perpetually on the calendar, even if it is a year away.
- Ideally, we should get away once in the spring and fall (after our kids' busy sports seasons).

Again, this might be the most exciting, refreshing news you get all day. If you are married, invest in that marriage with your time and your money. If it's not in your budget right now to get away for several days, look for options that fit your finances. Borrow a friend's place like we did, or head somewhere you know the costs will be lower. My friend's parents do a yearly "house trade" with their kids; the young couple comes to the parents' house, alone, for a little staycation, and the grandparents go to stay with the kids. Cheap and refreshing! Plan ahead and set aside what you can to treat yourselves in whatever way you can afford. It will pay off in big ways for your relationship.

6. Find some "couple friends."

Adulthood can be isolating, especially if you move to a new town. It takes about one hundred times more work and effort to find good friends after college. It took us a really long time to find good friends, and we had to work at it. Even if you manage *individually* to find close friends (which is certainly important), it can feel like an extreme impossibility to find friends *together*. There are so many hurdles to jump. The girl has to like the girl. The guy has to like the guy. Then those two people have to actually like you back enough to want to get together regularly. (We got stuck on this step for a while.) You have to mesh without it feeling awkward. And then you have to all be willing and able to invest The Most Valuable Commodity Parents Have: time! If this miracle does occur, hold on to these people for dear life. It will feel like a selfish luxury, but it absolutely is not.

We now have a group of couples who have been a lifeline for us. Todd and I feel most alive, as a couple, when we are having fun and serving alongside a group of friends, since we met doing just that when we were leaders in the ministry of Young Life. It makes us feel like we are young when we do these things now. I don't know what that special ingredient is for you. What makes you and your husband feel most alive? Who are the people you can be really real with? There is a definite sense of accountability in a group like this. You know you have people who will ask you (*plural* "you") hard questions. And there are people prompting you to get out, go places, look nice. I don't know about you, but my stay-at-home wardrobe game is not the strongest. It is a good thing to get out and look like a human once in a while.

NAVIGATING DECISIONS WHEN MOM AND DAD DISAGREE

Well, this isn't quite as fun, but it is an important aspect of building a strong family. Parents I surveyed commonly voiced this question: "How do you handle parenting decisions when you disagree?" This is the question, is it not? Currently my husband and I are in a little discussion about whether or not a certain gifted soccer player under our roof should play elite soccer three days a week, forty minutes away, or just be content with a happy little team in our hometown. TBD on this one. Of all the parenting decisions we'll face, this is probably one of the more minor. Couples genuinely wrestle over bigger questions like moving to a new home, homeschooling versus traditional school, consequences for certain behaviors, having another baby, holidays with extended family, and on and on! Even so, any time Mom and Dad disagree, it can make for a bumpy ride.

As I spoke with parents who had been married for many years, one theme that emerged was the importance of presenting a united front to children. No matter what sort of disagreements happen behind closed doors, it is vitally important that parents *appear* united when presenting parenting decisions. Kids are like hyenas, and if they see a weaker member of the herd, they'll surround them and prey on the unsuspecting beast. Well, that might be a bit dramatic, but you get the point! I've heard that you can share with your child about the disagreements between the two of you proportionally to the amount of maturity the kid displays. In other words, if you have an older, extremely mature child, the thinking is that you could selectively share a bit of the behind-the-scenes tension with this child. I think this makes sense, but I would personally advise extreme discretion here. A "mature" ten-year-old is probably not yet old enough for all this. Our oldest is fifteen. We have never really followed this advice, but I can see us saying something like this: "Buddy, we are talking about whether or not you'll play on that elite soccer team. Since soccer has been so important to Dad, he understands how you feel. We are still deciding what we will do." This would allow me to share a small amount of the tension, while also presenting the parents as the ultimate deciders and a separate, united front.

Obviously, what happens between a husband and wife when they disagree is a hugely nuanced and personal issue, and to address it thoroughly would be beyond the realm of this book. In my own experience as a wife and mother, I've found these decisions are easier the healthier the marriage is. When we are working heartily on all the things in this chapter (spending good time together, investing in the relationship, treating one another with respect, praying for strength to love one another), it helps make the times that we have to make serious decisions a little less tension filled.

Further, and I know this is a sticky issue, but I have personally seen a heap of blessing come into my life when I am overwhelmed with making a decision and let my husband make the call. I am not talking about times when I feel vehemently uncomfortable or opposed to something, but rather the times when I genuinely have no clue what to do. When I've worked myself up into a giant dither about a situation, and we've gone back and forth with pros and cons ad nauseam, and I'm starting to feel this intense emotional stress, it is a giant relief to say to Todd, "You know what? This is yours. You make this call." Perhaps this is not a piece of didactic instruction but more of an anecdotal observation? But I would be remiss not to share; this has brought relief and blessing to our family more times than I can count.

Similarly, I so appreciate that Todd often defers to me when it's an area I feel strongly about, or have researched thoroughly. I think it's an equal blessing to him that there is a long list of things about which he will never have to decide.

STRENGTH TO PARENT WHEN YOU FEEL ALONE

As I mentioned earlier, I realize that not everyone has a strong marriage. Maybe your marriage, like my Grammy's, is a source of more stress than strength. Maybe you even find yourself in a position you never expected—parenting alone as a single parent. If so, my friend Lauren, an incredible single mom, has some wise words for you:

"It's hard to stay upbeat and positive when raising kids as a single parent, but I think it's so important. Sometimes after a divorce, especially if it's unwanted, there is a tendency to play the victim. . . . Focusing on what you *do* have, instead of what you don't have—this is the most important thing for a single mom. It can be tempting to think about the life you've lost, and how easy things used to be. But that's not helpful, healthy, productive, or biblical. We are more than conquerors! We are to remember that God is the God of the hills *and* the valleys. And when you stop and look at it, you still have a lot! You still have your kids, your health, your family."

I absolutely love her positivity! Of course, I am sure that even with the most amazing attitude, it still stinks to largely parent alone. We need help. Lauren encourages single moms to keep connected with others. "There's a tendency to shrink back from social situations, like church, because you don't want to go alone," she says. "Keep plugging in, keep volunteering, still put your kids in sports if you can. I have to ask for help sometimes, and I hate it. But I need it. My kids were young when we split. People are willing to help if you ask. (And you need to return the favor!) When people know what you're dealing with, they will want to help, but that requires you being honest and vulnerable about what you're going through."

Whether you are braving a difficult marriage or no marriage, or even if you find yourself in a grumpy state of things about your marriage (perhaps retreating to Target to shop for underwear, like yours truly)—no matter how alone you might feel in your circumstances, keep connected with others and lean on Jesus. We might feel that we have no one to rely on, but we are never alone!

SUMMING IT UP

- Strong marriages help build strong families.
- But you don't need a strong marriage to build a strong family.
- If you're married, prioritize fun together!

TALKING IT OVER

1. If you're married, what's your biggest challenge as a couple in this season of life?
2. If you're married, what was the most life-giving trip or date you and your husband have taken?

COMING HOME

Think of a couple you respect. Ask them how they prioritize their marriage in busy seasons.

5

PRAYER

Because Parenting Makes You Desperate

The criteria for coming to Jesus is weariness. Come overwhelmed with life. Come with your wandering mind. Come messy.

PAUL E. MILLER, *A Praying Life*

Okay. So far we have discussed four prerequisites for building a strong family: honesty, perspective, authority, and partnership. This next one might actually be the most important: prayer.

I don't know what your religious beliefs are. Maybe you've picked up this book because you're intrigued by the concept of building a strong family, but you're not quite with me on the whole "prayer" thing. As I said in the introduction, I welcome you here. For me, prayer is an important part of the strength of my family for one reason: I simply am not enough. Not strong enough, not present enough, not smart enough, not organized enough, not wise enough . . . just not *enough*. When I think about what it takes to raise a strong family, it is simply too big of a job. It is in these times that I am grateful to have Someone walking with me—Someone who is all of those things I am not.

WHEN GOD ANSWERS PRAYERS

One of the most desperate times for Todd and me was the season after our first son was born. He cried for hours, and not a normal baby cry—a deep, painful, hysterical *scream*. As the months dragged on, he wouldn't make eye contact and he wasn't babbling. Our pediatrician was concerned and referred us to developmental specialists. For us as new parents, this was earth-shattering. We were already overwhelmed in our new role ("we" = basically me). To be only so far into parenting and already be facing these sorts of challenges and questions . . . I was shaken to my core, and Todd was doing the best that he could to steady the ship, although he was rattled himself.

After that pediatrician visit, we sent an email to every Christian we knew. We described the problem with our baby and begged people to pray. One person I sent the email to was an older lady, a mom of two grown sons. Of all the replies, hers is the one I have never forgotten: "Jessica, I will pray. God has always been so faithful with my boys, and He will be with your son too." After twenty years of parenting, she knew. Now, I'm still a baby in learning to trust the Lord, and even a baby in parenting (only fifteen years in), but even today, I could see myself responding to an email in the same way that woman did. God has been so faithful.

Shortly after we sent that email desperate for prayer, we discovered my son's food allergies. A few days on a new diet, and he was a completely different baby. Not just a little better, but a completely different, cheerful, babbling child. It never gets old to think about it.

It was a really fun exercise to reach out to friends and ask them for examples of God's answered prayers for their families. My, the stories that poured in! I love this story from my friend Lynn: "One wintry day my in-laws were driving to visit us. It was about a seven-hour drive. During the day, it started snowing really bad, and our son John, who was about five or six, came into the kitchen and announced that we really ought to pray for Gramma and Doodad. We prayed together for their safety, and when they arrived, several hours later, they recounted that they had a scary incident on the thruway. Their car spun out of control, and they ended up in the median. They were amazed that they hadn't hit any other cars. When we asked them what time that happened, it was right when John said we needed to pray!" I love that God used the prayers of a child to show this family His care and provision.

My friend Angela said, "When our daughter was born, she had a kidney that did not function. At eleven months, they removed her kidney without incident. Two months later, a golf-ball-sized lump appeared on her abdomen. The surgeon said it was a hernia that would have to be repaired. 'These things don't repair themselves,' he said. So we scheduled her for her second surgery in less than three months! This one I was not prepared for. We had prayed and prayed and now felt unheard. The day came for the surgery, and the surgeon came in to mark her abdomen. He stopped when he saw her and said, 'Mom, I think this looks smaller than it did four weeks ago.' He put off the surgery for six weeks. Six weeks later when we saw him in his office, the hernia was completely gone! Thirty-two years later, I keep a pink surgical marker to remind me that God does indeed answer prayers, even when we think He is not listening."

And because I can't resist, here's another fun story about the adoption of our dear friend Joshua. His mom says: "In the adoption process, we had a LOT of paperwork to get done within a certain time. It would cause incredible delays if we got behind. There was a big, important set of financial papers that we had been waiting for my husband's work to complete. He had called and called, and no one knew where it was. He suspected that it was in the office of an employee who had been out for over a week. We prayed about it often. On the night before the paperwork was due, my husband and a coworker were in that office building, but the room where he thought the paperwork was located was locked. Then his coworker's dog pooped on the floor (yes, poop was the key!), and they had to find cleaning supplies. His coworker accidentally found a way into the office Nathan had tried to get into. She found cleaning supplies, and he found our paperwork—all ready to go!"

Gosh, if you're like me, you love these little stories. I got goose bumps reading all of them, reminded of the ways God shows up in the minuscule details of our lives.

WHEN GOD DOESN'T ANSWER PRAYERS

While these true stories are wonderful, life doesn't always tie up so perfectly. I know what it's like to have answered prayers, but I also know what it's like to have unanswered ones that seem to bounce off of the ceiling and thud on the floor. We've been praying for fifteen years for God to heal my son's food allergies. After all, He could do it in a second. *This* second.

But He hasn't.

My friend Rachel knows something about this too. She has walked through something I cannot imagine and understands the depths of suffering in a way that I cannot. At age four, Rachel's daughter, Taylor, was diagnosed with a rare genetic neurologically degenerative disease called Sanfilippo syndrome, often referred to as "childhood Alzheimer's." During Taylor's childhood, she suffered even while Rachel prayed. And yet, in the midst of unanswered prayer, Rachel's faith inspires us all. She writes:

> God is big enough to contend with your sorrow. His arms are wide enough to hold you in your pain. Pain cannot grip you tighter than God's grace. . . . His answer to your prayer is not 'no' for denial's sake. Instead, *because* of His

> mercy, grace, great love for us, and sovereign plan for each of us, He issues 'no's' that we can't perceive because we can't predict the future. He can. He will hold you fast and never let go; His love goes beyond the no. His arms are wide enough to hold every broken heart.[1]

Powerful words from a mother who has been in a pit of terror and grief such that many of us cannot imagine. Even in our family's own unanswered prayers for our son's allergies, we can still see that God has been good. I hate the allergies, but this struggle really makes us rely on Him in a way we wouldn't otherwise. I can see how He's using this unwanted thing to grow our character, to grow our son's character. He's not giving us exactly what we want, but He gives us what we need, day by day.

PRAYING WHILE PARENTING

Maybe it's my doubt . . . or laziness . . . But if I'm honest with you, for much of my life, prayer was not important. It was a bonus sort of thing, something I tacked on at the end of a quiet time because that's what Christians do, right? They pray?

Then I became a mom. Parenting made me desperate, and desperation makes us pray. Real prayers, that is—bold and needy ones. Now, praying often feels like this: "God. You need to show up here. You have to. You are the only hope we have."

When I became a mom, someone gave me a blue polka-dot blanket at a baby shower. On the blanket it said, "For this child I have prayed," which is a verse from the Old Testament. It comes from 1 Samuel, where a barren woman named Hannah had prayed for a child, and God heard her prayer.[2] Well, I have to tell you, I felt a little funny reading those words at the baby shower. After all, Todd and I had not exactly been praying for a child, at least not specifically. Our first baby was a total surprise, and although we were thrilled to be parents, the verse felt like it wasn't exactly relevant. (Narrator: But it would become very relevant.)

Once we learned that my son had life-threatening food allergies—and asthma as well—it felt like we lived on our knees. For this child we have prayed. And prayed and prayed. When our son had his most recent allergic reaction (at age fourteen), I posted on Instagram from the hospital room: "You're never really 'out of the woods' with food allergies. You live in the woods." The desperation never really leaves. I know this sounds weird, but when we're getting ready to start a meal, and something about it makes me nervous—my son coughs for an unknown reason, someone new is preparing his food, there's a new ingredient, it's an unsafe, allergy-filled environment—I often feel as if I cannot breathe. It's in these moments I go to the only place where you can be by yourself for a minute and not arouse questions: the bathroom.

I often meet God in the bathroom. I will squat down in a corner (avoiding touching the floor, because obviously, germs). I will take a breath and say, "God, You have to show up here. If You don't, he won't be safe." It is not a request as much as a stated fact.

Paul E. Miller says it best in *A Praying Life*:

> It took me seventeen years to realize I couldn't parent on my own. It was not a great spiritual insight, just a realistic observation. If I didn't pray deliberately and reflectively for members of my family by name every morning, they'd kill one another. I was incapable of getting inside their hearts. I was desperate. . . .
>
> God answered my prayer. As I began to pray regularly for the children, he began to work in their hearts. . . . It didn't take me long to realize I did my best parenting by prayer. I began to speak less to the kids and more to God. It was actually quite relaxing.[3]

I think that sometimes the reason we moms don't pray well is that we don't understand how badly our families need us to pray. It seems to me the great men and women of faith were people of prayer and that they also had people praying for them. In Cindy Rollins's memoir, *Beyond Mere Motherhood*, she writes about her mother-in-law:

> Helen had a simple faith that meant one thing: a life of prayer. She prayed for her family. She never had the money to travel much to see her large family after they grew up. We often only saw her once every couple of years. But whenever we talked to her on the phone, she reminded us that she was praying for us. I didn't share with her all the struggles I faced over the years when I was pregnant or nursing, but she had borne six children, and she knew. Just when I felt I was about to be overwhelmed and washed away by life, she would call and tell me she was praying for me. By the end of my childbearing years, I clung to her prayers, like a drowning man to a raft. When I couldn't pray, she could. When I had no faith, she did. When she died, I felt like a giant black hole opened in the universe. Who was going to pray now? Well, it was obvious. I was going to have to step up to the plate.[4]

If we don't pray, it's because we just don't see things for how they truly are. As we are raising children in these crazy times, prayer for our families is vital. We must be a generation of mothers on our knees. We must see the need and know the power. We are here for such a time as this—we are here to pray. To pray for our families. Our prayers matter. We pray for the big things and the little things. We pray for His will to be done. We pray for protection from the evil one.

One hymn that I can hardly ever make it through without

crying is "What a Friend We Have in Jesus." These words are as true today as when they were written in 1855. I hope they are a comfort to you today as you parent. Whatever you are facing, you do not have to face it alone.

What a Friend we have in Jesus,
All our sins and griefs to bear!
What a privilege to carry
Everything to God in prayer!

O what peace we often forfeit,
O what needless pain we bear,
All because we do not carry
Everything to God in prayer![5]

SUMMING IT UP

- We can always pray in our times of need. God never tires of hearing from us.
- Our families need us to pray.

TALKING IT OVER

1. Is it easy or difficult for you to believe that God answers prayer? Why?
2. When was a time that God answered prayers for your family?
3. When was a time that God didn't answer your prayers in the way that you hoped?

COMING HOME

Read Paul E. Miller's *A Praying Life* and consider implementing his prayer card system.[6] Life-changing!

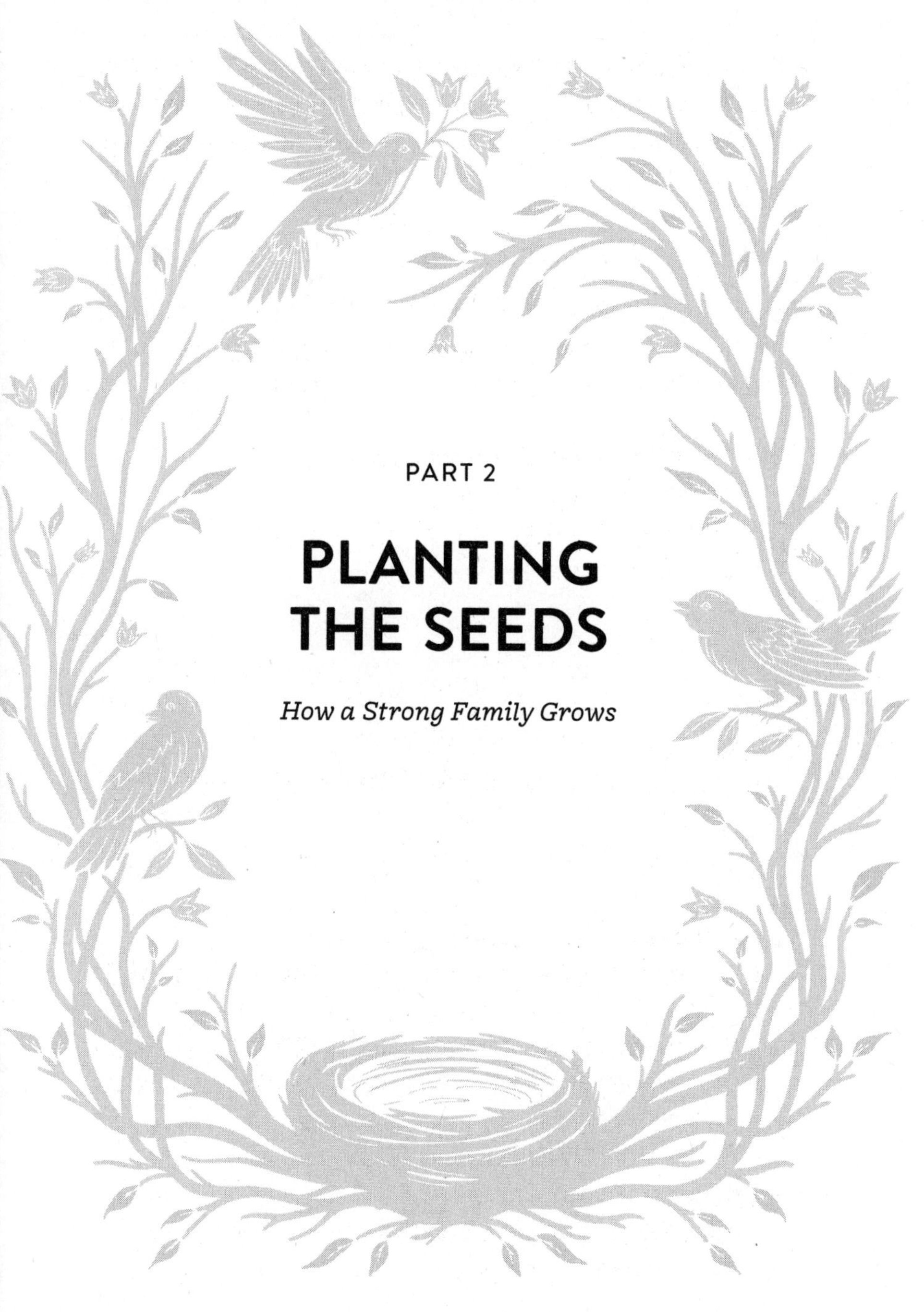

PART 2

PLANTING THE SEEDS

How a Strong Family Grows

6

TIME

On Sports, Phones, and Family Dinner

I have a personal advantage in having lived for sixty years. . . . I can say positively that the years fly past like a mist in the night! Time disappears more quickly than smoke! It is not possible to go backwards. The "now" is important if there is ever to be any family life.

EDITH SCHAEFFER, *What Is a Family?*

Three years ago, we sold our house in the most amazing neighborhood to build on thirty acres with my family. At the time we were first considering it, I had mixed feelings. One reason for this was the thought of moving away from my friend Page, who is one of God's sweetest gifts to me. Page was my neighbor for ten years in our old neighborhood. She is the type of friend who throws on her size four Lululemons and runs three miles the week after she has a baby (PUSHING THE STROLLER), but she is so nice you don't hate her for it, not even a little bit.

The first day Page moved in, she bopped in my door with a load of wet laundry because her dryer was broken. The house filled with her laughter, and for the next ten years her joy lit up my life. She was the foil to my postpartum depression and to several episodes where I silently or not-so-silently mourned my imminent (yet never materializing) diagnoses from multiple diseases. So many days I would be in the pits of some terrible internal trauma, and I would force myself to heat up my cold coffee and bring it across the street. I pretended it was because I needed an egg, but really it was because I was drowning in darkness and she was light. Her cheery "Hello!" would ground me. Our families had so many memories together from sunset games of "yolf" (yard golf), watching kids dance around in diapers (or no diapers; one time her toddler son pooped in our garage, and I never went barefoot in there again). We moved out of that neighborhood within a month of one another. The night her family moved away, I sat in the front yard and wept until my eyes were swollen.

Since moving apart, we have remained friends, but a scheduled coffee date is different from going over to borrow a strapless bra and commiserating because someone just put waterproof mascara on your brand-new white comforter from Pottery Barn. (Which happened!!) She will always be my friend. It is just not quite the same now.

There is a reason for this. *And that reason is time.*

Time is a thing that matters. The people that you spend time with are the people you are closest to. And that is just true. Since I am an Enneagram 6 (a "loyalist"), I have a really hard time with seasons ending and friendships changing. I want things to always and forever be the same, but I have learned that God gives us what we need when we need it. I now have a wonderful "bonus" neighbor named Jacquelyn, and I guess God knew that we needed each other. She is a new gift because of shared time. (She's also cheery and not a hypochondriac, which is good because a neighborhood needs only one of those at a time.)

THE POWER OF TIME

Time isn't just the thing that builds friendships—it also builds families. One study asked over 1,500 schoolkids, "What makes a happy family?" Strangely absent were mentions of Disneyland vacations or anything material. The prevailing answer was: a strong family is a family that does things together and enjoys spending time together.[1] Did you hear it? *Time.* I don't remember where I heard the cheesy saying, "Kids spell love T-I-M-E." Cheesy, but true!

In another oft repeated phrase, both *quantity* and *quality* time are important. Author and researcher Dr. Nick Stinnett conducted a research project involving three thousand families. He found that one of the key links in strong families was time. The study revealed, "Happy families spend time together, not only quality time but quantity time. They work, they plan, they struggle, and they play together."[2]

I don't want this chapter to cause guilt, but rather to motivate us and keep us pointed in the right direction. I left my kids this morning to write this book. There are decisions to make and days we don't spend quantity or quality time together. This isn't all-or-nothing, a thing that is achieved and mastered once, but something we parents have to constantly ponder as we navigate life in the twenty-first century. There have never been so many threats to a family who want to spend time together, the main ones being activities, people, and technology. Let's unpack some wisdom for addressing these three arenas.

Choose Activities Wisely

There was a year that Todd and I realized both of our sons were good at baseball, and this was an irresistible allure into a life we never planned to live. On Saturdays, for a relentless ten months of the year, one of us would drive with one son an hour away to sit behind left field for eight hours, and the other one of us would drive an hour in the other direction, with the other son, to sit behind a different left field. Many weekends it was Sunday too. I never could believe that there was not a conglomeration of ten players at an appropriate ability level in our own hometown that our sons could compete against, but nevertheless, we obediently drove our sons to various locales, repeatedly, and separately. Most times, one of us also dragged along our daughter, whom we pacified with sticker books and the occasional thirteen-dollar shaved ice.

God rescued us out of this life when one son inexplicably did not make even one of three possible teams. We were devastated. He, weirdly, was not. The other son broke his foot and his season got cut short. We were devastated. He, weirdly, was not. Of course, there were gifts from the season of travel baseball, and parts of it that I do miss. Yet, for our family, I am abundantly grateful God intervened and it ended.

You do need to know that we didn't quit sports; we switched sports. God provided a way for my two sons to play soccer together, on the same team—a gift on many levels. And even though all three of our kids could be playing higher levels, more games, on better teams, our current situation works for our family. Maybe we will regret chasing soccer excellence with only a medium amount of investment. Maybe they will regret it. I don't know. What I do know is that our family enjoys being together, and this allows us to do that.

The villain of this story is not travel baseball. (Although, #teamsoccer.) In Cindy Rollins's motherhood memoir, *Beyond Mere Motherhood*, she looks back with wistful eyes on years spent on the baseball field, as a mom of nine children, eight of whom are sons. The real villain is any Big Thing our family will regret years later because of what it cost us versus what it gave us. When I look back on the baseball years, it was a season of our family saying yes to everyone and everything—including things off the field. Yes, I will be your children's ministry director. And serve on this committee and that one. Yes, we will host a Young Life table and a book club. Yes, I will write a book. And another book. Yes, we will go on that trip, and another trip, and then another trip. Yes, we will do that playdate group and do piano and flag football and dance. All the things! We would have crashed and burned if left to our own devices. Some of us nearly did.

Every family is different. You have to decide what's right for your family. However, here are some principles I would submit for consideration if you parent talented kids and you also value quality and quantity family time:

1. *The Interest Question.* What is the ratio of your child's actual interest in the activity to the cost on the family? (PS: Ask your kids how much they like things. I am often surprised that their excitement is vastly less than I thought it was.) One time my cousin's son (who was a key player on a high-level, elite team) told him, "Dad, I'd actually just rather go to church and play on the farm on the weekends than do baseball tournaments. Can I do that?"
2. *The Mealtime Question.* How many family meals are you able to eat together with this commitment, and does this reflect your values?
3. *The Whole Family Question.* Put yourselves in the shoes of the other siblings. What do their lives look like? Are they consistently feeling as if they're being dragged around to watch a more talented sibling perform? What might that feel like? Do they seem perpetually fussy at said activities? Can you blame them? Are you asking them to do something you wouldn't want to do yourself? It doesn't necessarily mean that you shouldn't Do the Thing, but the answers to these questions can guide you in how to intentionally make sure the whole family is cared for.

4. *The Motivation Question.* This is a hard one. Am I as a parent secretly getting something out of this activity? Does it help me avoid being in a house that's totally disorganized? Does it fulfill my need to have a successful kid? Do I really like being with other parents? None of these are reasons to say no. But it's good to be honest about why we do what we do and not just sign up for something because "she always does dance" or "they asked him to play." As I mentioned, travel baseball was only half the problem for us. Well, maybe more than half. But it certainly was not the only choice we made that led us to a life of overwhelm. I'm a person who likes being busy.

The point of this chapter isn't "Don't do things." The point of the chapter is "Be wise. Families take time." Activities, because they cost time, directly affect the friendships your family is able to build. What I didn't know at first was that everything has a cost.

When you sign up to take someone a meal, for example, it costs not only extra dollars for more spinach and chicken, but extra time to plan the meal, arrange the drop-off, make the extra food, and deliver it. Not to mention the mess of getting everyone in the car and back out of the car. You will be more stressed on these days. You will have less bandwidth for handling your kids' arguments or questions. I am beyond grateful for the people who have brought me meals in hard times. I am so glad they did. I am not saying don't take meals or be on committees. I am saying be sure you count the hidden costs first.

In his highly respected study, Stinnett found that "When outside pressures (work, for example) threaten to remove family from its top priority, members of strong families take action and make sacrifices if necessary to preserve family well-being."[3] It reminds me of a story in *The Meaning of Marriage*. Coauthor Kathy Keller's husband, the renowned pastor Tim Keller, was in a season of overwork. Although he had repeatedly promised Kathy that after a couple of months he would step back on his commitments, those months came and went, and still the family rarely saw him. Kathy got so desperate that when he came home one night, he found her smashing her fine china on the balcony of their high-rise New York apartment. It was her way of making the point that Tim was throwing something just as valuable out the window. Tim reflects that this desperate action got his attention. Kathy cared enough to do something drastic.[4] Don't be afraid to do something drastic if it saves your family.

Be Strategic About Time Spent with Other People

Friends are a good thing, right? Yes—in moderation. Another way to protect family time is to be conscious of who is around, and how often. If there are always other people present, your family doesn't have time to sufficiently develop its own story.

In Edith Schaeffer's wonderful book *What Is a Family?* she defines family as "an open door with hinges and a lock."[5] Now, if you know anything about Edith Schaeffer, you could definitely not accuse her of being inhospitable! In contrast, the Schaeffers made it their life mission to open their door to seekers at their L'Abri Fellowship in Switzerland. This sweet little chalet hosted thousands of visitors over the years, serving meals, ministering to hearts. At the same time, Edith says of the family, "The hinges should be well-oiled to swing the door open during certain times, but the lock should be firm enough to let people know that the family needs to be alone part of the time, just to *be* a family."[6]

Edith gets practical about what this looked like for them: "In addition to the one day a week [a family day], certain hours or at least one hour of each day should be given by one of the two parents—unbroken time, not to be interrupted—for the children or one child alone to read books, talk over their questions, read the Bible portion of the day, and pray together. No matter what visitor is in your home, he or she can wait for that hour to be up."[7] I think it's astounding that in the midst of all of the "good things" this woman was doing—entertaining guests and sharing the gospel—she fiercely fought to preserve family time.

I am no Edith Schaeffer, but I have my own sorts of fights for family time. An interesting thing happens when your kids live on a plot of land with their cousins a hundred feet away. They often do not want to come home. I'm super glad for the cousin crew and that my kids can walk to my parents'. However, every so often I'll get a nudge that we need a minute, that our own family needs some time.

As a result, I have been known to, for no specific reason at all, collect all of my children from the fun places they are on this farm-neighborhood, gather them in the living room, and say, "We are just going to be in our house. To play with each other for a while." You will be shocked to know this is highly unpopular. You would have thought I canceled Christmas. "Mom!!! Why?" (Read this in the whiniest nine-year-old voice.) And I will say something like "Guys, we've been going hard for the past week. We've all been doing a lot of things, and we need some time in our own house with one another."

(Cue more whining at the massive injustice that has just occurred.)

Why would I do this? Why would any mom who had previously been enjoying a peaceful, empty house voluntarily invoke such torment and suffering upon herself and her loved ones? I have asked myself the same question. But the reason that I land on is something akin to this: family, like friendship, takes time. Most great friendships are forged in the doldrums of life, where you end up talking about nothing and everything, being bored, having awkward silence and not-so-awkward silence, playing everyday games, working alongside one another. Time isn't the only ingredient for a friendship, but you definitely can't cook one up without it.

Are your kids always in different places? Is your family running at 100 mph to separate events? Are Mom and Dad regularly gone three or four nights a week while the kids eat chicken nuggets alone at the counter? Do you bring random kids on vacation with you? Maybe don't. Maybe just be bored and together on purpose. By choice. Even when it's widely unpopular.

Monitor Technology Use Carefully

Okay, now the biggie. I think the worst threat to family time is technology, specifically the smartphone. The effects of phones on our youngest, most susceptible generation are becoming impossible to ignore. Jonathan Haidt, author of *The Anxious Generation*, claims, "Our children are going on a conveyor belt. . . . And a lot of them are getting shredded."[8] Haidt particularly calls out TikTok: "TikTok is able to train behavior the way a dog trainer trains a dog with tiny little rewards for tiny action. As I'm discovering from talking to my students, short-form videos of the kind pioneered by TikTok are the most addictive, the most narcotic. They put you into kind of a mesmerized state, much like a slot machine addict. TikTok is a platform that young people themselves say they wish didn't exist."[9]

Haidt observes that the tech crisis is affecting our boys and girls differently. While girls are suffering from intense, unprecedented rates of anxiety, boys are just dropping out of life. He says the digital life is causing boys "to drop out of life, not cultivate skills, like flirting or courtship or working for pay. It's causing them to drop out of life in ways that will block their flourishing for the rest of their lives."[10]

I have observed this trend in real time. I've noticed kids in our community seem less interested in dating, hanging out, getting their driver's licenses, applying for jobs, playing games, being outside. I do not think it's hyperbole to say that technology addiction is re-forming, remaking, undoing the youngest generation, producing human beings who won't be able to have normal sex lives, normal conversations, deep friendships, or close-knit families.

If we want to stop this trend from affecting our families, we need to look different. *Weird*, even. As I mentioned in the introduction, this can actually be a huge asset to building a strong family. Our kids can think: *I'm not alone! There are more weird ones like me at home!*

As far as what "being weird" looks like in the area of technology, I have quite a bit of experience, mainly because iPhone addiction is an area of personal struggle for me. I have many days where I'm proud of myself, and many where I have to repent and try again tomorrow.

One thing I am so grateful we did is delay giving our kids phones. My oldest is fifteen and has no phone. This makes him basically a unicorn. But especially as more and more studies emerge on the impact of technology, I become more solidified in our choice. Even Gen Z young people say they will place much stricter limits on their kids' phone use.[11] I do believe a countermovement is forming; I hope and pray the tide is shifting.

When we do give our kids phones, they will not be wrapped up like a present for a special occasion. My phone is largely not a gift to me; it's a tool to steward wisely, and a temptation to fight. So when my kids do have to have a phone, I will call it what it is and not put a bow on it, literally or figuratively.

And then they get to follow the example we have set for them. This is hugely motivational . . . and deeply convicting. As I suffer from major iPhone self-control issues, I've had to implement all sorts of little systems to help me. For example, I have time blocks on my phone for my vices. I get ten minutes a day on Instagram, and if I want more, I have to enter a password (which only my husband knows). This is a neat little trick, except when you're at the Verizon store and need to call your husband to unlock something while you're standing at the counter and therefore you look like a Complete Weirdo. It is mostly a very effective system. I do not have Facebook on my phone. If I want to go on Facebook, I have to sit at the desktop computer in our schoolroom, where my children will probably come up behind me and ask, "Who is that person?" at least seventeen times, so this takes most of the fun out of it.

I also aim to not be on my phone on family road trips, instead just being bored along with my kids. (When my husband is driving, that is; of course, I'm not on my phone while I'm driving!) In a similar vein, we also don't have phones at the dinner table. Hard stop. When I'm with someone one-on-one, I put away my phone. I am definitely addicted, but I am aware of it and fight it hard. Oh, and here's one last little tip if you get really desperate: this year I told the kids I would give them a dollar every time I was on the phone during our homeschool hours. I would describe this as a very effective and highly annoying way to break a habit.

Despite all these systems, I still struggle. I just find myself doing way too much checking. I don't even know what I am checking for sometimes. I am just checking. I have discovered I am most susceptible when I am tired. I really have to put my guard up then.

As much as I would like to have a silver bullet solution to handling technology, I don't think there is one, except that we have to fight and keep fighting. Keep plodding along, as Cindy Rollins says.[12]

I recognize that technology is a hot-button issue that stirs differing opinions, even among spouses. And yet I believe handling it well is tremendously important to building a strong family. You can have the calmest schedule ever, eat family dinner each night, hang out regularly, but if someone is present but not really *present*, it doesn't matter, does it?

If you've been looking for affirmation to not give your kids a phone, Snapchat, or a gaming system, here is your sign! Sometimes I wish someone would take away *my* iPhone so I could concentrate on what matters! If you're looking for someone to tell you that your kids can be in high school and not have a phone or social media and be completely content—they can! (Homeschooling definitely helps.) It is very hard to un-give technology. Hold out for as long as possible. And for the technology your kids do have—don't you dare be afraid to set boundaries, delete apps, unplug systems. If you need to be reminded you're not the only weird mom out there—you're not! Your kids want you—they *need* you—to save them from themselves and guide them through the craziness.

PRIORITIZE FAMILY MEALS

We've talked about the challenges to family time—activities, people, technology. Now, we're going to end on a positive, as we deep dive into perhaps the most impactful thing that you could do together: family dinner!

We know that eating meals as a family is important. But besides the fact that I *feel* good about sitting down together, do family dinners really *do* anything? In study after study, family meals are linked to about every positive outcome you could imagine. More frequent family meals are linked to lower anxiety and depression in kids, lower rates of eating disorders, increased vocabularies, healthier eating habits when kids are grown, less chance of getting addicted to drugs or alcohol, higher self-esteem, and significantly higher success in school![13] Wow! All of those positive things, just by sitting down to eat enchiladas together! And no stress if the enchiladas aren't gourmet; in a recent study, 71 percent of teens said their favorite part of family meals was the ability to listen and talk with their family members—in other words, it had nothing to do with the food.[14]

Now is the part where I tell you that we eat dinner as a family together every night, because, obviously. Except . . . we do not. We usually eat a special breakfast together on Saturday and Sunday, even if it has to be early, or late . . . And then we eat probably two or three dinners together as a family during the week. We have to fight for each one. It was easier when the kids were younger and activities fewer, but it was also more stressful. It is hard to do quality bonding when half of the table wants to argue about garbage trucks and you spend every two minutes retrieving the sippy cup from the floor. Here is what I have learned over the years about family dinners.

1. Don't compare yourself to some real or imagined ideal. Start this week. Attempt one more meal together. Five is better than four. One is better than none.

2. Be willing to plan it and then protect it. If I can see that we are insanely busy for the next two weeks, I find a night or two that will work for family dinner, write it down on the calendar, and treat it like any other social event. We don't feel bad about saying no to something else. Family dinner is worth fighting for.

3. Be flexible. Yummy breakfast counts. Lunch counts. Eating at 8:00 p.m. counts, even if everyone has had enough snacks at that point to constitute dinner.

4. Try to make it as special as you can. *Important note:* sometimes in life this will rightly mean "not special at all." If you are hanging on by a thread, do not impose guilt on yourself for a frozen pizza or a carton of Chick-fil-A nuggets shared

at the table. But. If you don't feel like life is running you over with a cement mixer, consider using some of your surplus energy to make dinner a little nicer. Your family dinner should not always get the leftovers, literally or figuratively.

5. Attempt to keep the conversation pleasant. Sometimes in my childhood, my mom would take this really long pause and let out a deep sigh before saying the dinnertime prayer. I always thought that was odd. Now I realize she was calming her blood pressure and praying for strength to make it through dinner. She saw the virtue of keeping mealtimes pleasant and not merely using them as a platform to give the behavioral lectures that have been storing up over the day. Even as I write this, I am convicted that I need to chill out on the "table manners fight" I have been waging over the past few dinners with one son.

Leonard Sax sums it up well: "We have to fight for supper with our families. Fight for time with your child. Cancel or forego afterschool activities, if need be, in order to have more evening meals together. Your kids can't attach to you if they hardly ever see you. And turn the devices off."[15]

I love practical suggestions, so I have included some super-doable ideas for family meals! See the sidebars for help with answering that age-old question "What's for dinner?" I hope these lists will be helpful next time you're in a slump and want to create some magic at the dinner table.

Whether it's by being intentional about family dinners or by carefully monitoring our family's activity level, involvement with other people, and use of technology, we can have an incredible impact on our family's time together. When we make time for our kids, we are building a strong family.

Favorite Family Cookbooks

- *Return to Sunday Dinner* by Russell Cronkhite
- *The America's Test Kitchen Family Cookbook*
- *Sunday Suppers* by Cynthia Graubart
- *Magnolia Table* cookbooks
- *Danielle Walker's Against All Grain Celebrations* (gluten-free, dairy-free, and paleo)

Favorite Family Meals

Here's a roundup of ideas that can make a meal special, whether purchased or homemade.

- Breakfast for dinner
- Burger bowls
- Steak and oven fries
- BBQ ribs and corn bread
- Pizza night
- Greek grilled chicken or kebabs, hummus and pitas, cucumbers, tomatoes, rice, olives
- Beef stew or pot roast and apple pie
- Chicken pot pie
- Chicken Caesar salad with all the toppings
- Fettuccine Alfredo with homemade rolls
- Bourbon chicken fried rice
- Shepherd's pie
- Steak and bacon-wrapped shrimp
- Stroganoff with meatballs
- Chicken Parmesan
- Pot roast with sourdough
- Chicken broccoli Alfredo
- Anything with place mats and lit candles!

Ways to Make Dinner Special

- From a reader: to get kids to stay at the table longer, light a candle, and whoever finishes their full meal first gets to blow out the candle!
- Print off some conversation starters. Find many free online for all ages.
- From my sister-in-law Julianne: leave your Christmas candles out during winter dinners to add a cozy hue to dark days.
- Have kids name their "high/low of the day."
- Have a red plate just for the kid who has done something special.

SUMMING IT UP

- Kids spell love "T-I-M-E."
- Some activities cost the family more than they return.
- Sometimes the family needs time just with one another.

TALKING IT OVER

1. What was your favorite meal as a child?
2. Do you feel that your family has too much time together at this stage of life, or not enough?
3. If you could do something over with regard to your family's use of technology, what would it be?

COMING HOME

1. Ask your kids what they think strong families do.
2. Read the list of yummy family dinners to the nearest kid. Let him or her choose the one you'll make next.
3. Look at the calendar and plan one family night in the next month. If you need more ideas to get your wheels turning, check appendix 2 for "Family Bonding Ideas."

One Family's Story: The Belks

Catherine and Hudson are some of our dearest friends. I love how they prioritize making memories and missional living while juggling a busy family schedule.

We've been married for seventeen years and have three daughters, ages seven, nine, and eleven. We've had seasons of homeschooling, but right now everyone is in public school. Hudson is in full-time ministry, and I'm a nurse practitioner. In some seasons I can gratefully scale back, but in this current one, I am working full-time. Our kids are very busy with sports and dance. Because life can get crazy, we have to be intentional about the things that matter to us.

We commit to having dinner together as a family at least four times a week, even if we have to eat before or after practices. We are consistent with family worship and Bible study, usually after dinner. As we plan our activities for the year, we try to keep a few nights of the week where we don't leave the home and go do separate things. That allows us one night to have a special family dinner, one for Hudson and me to have a date, and one for us to have people in the home for dinner. We try to take at least three vacations a year as a family where we get away and disconnect, even if it's a shorter time. It's often been Disney World, because we all enjoy that! We're always looking for ways to make memories with our kids, and this often involves sports. Pickup kickball games, snow days, family walks, and more.

One thing that was foundational for Hudson and me growing up was the way that our families were both very hospitable. We want our kids to see our home as a place to love and serve others. We have the kids' friends over as often as we can to join in with our family, even joining in on the family devotional in the evening. For the past few years, we've run Bible studies in our home for their friends—kids from the neighborhood or from their school. We try to talk about our faith as often as possible, not in a rote way, but just to bring it to life—when we're going to practice, going to school, engaging our neighbors, we hope that they see the reason we do things is that we try to follow Jesus.

Sometimes our kids travel for soccer tournaments. We try to use this time intentionally. We'll say to the team, "Hey, we're going to do a chapel or a Bible study in the hotel room. Who wants to come?" We've had ten to eleven girls come and as many parents.

We have a lot of different ideas and hopes about doing ministry as a family, but it starts with asking, "Who are we as a family? Who has God made us? Where has He placed us?" We look around where we are and try to move into those places, as a family, for the gospel.

7

CONNECTION

The Love Language of Syrup (and Other Ways to Stay Close in a Noisy World)

It is when things are the roughest that we should be holding on to our children the most firmly.

GORDON NEUFELD AND GABOR MATÉ
Hold On to Your Kids

In my first book, *Memory-Making Mom,*[1] I noted that as my siblings and I were growing up, we each thought we were my mom's favorite. This passing comment stuck out to a friend of mine, who later told me, "I would love to read a book on that. How did she do it? I feel so overwhelmed trying to love everyone equally." I have heard other moms express similar longings. I don't know for sure what was behind my friend's comment, but I've thought of some reasons this might be a common refrain:

1. We don't always feel equally warm toward all of our children, and we want a cure for this undesired feeling.
2. We felt unseen or "less than" in our family of origin and don't want our kids to ever feel this way.
3. It is clear that there is not enough "us" to go around for all of "them," and we hope for a secret cure to spread ourselves sufficiently.

We instinctively understand that family dinners are great and traditions are fun, but it is essential for each kid to feel that they are connected to the family and that they belong. Here we will attempt to tackle this motherhood dilemma, with some ideas for connecting with your kids individually. As I've thought about this topic, I've become even more resolved that each of my kids feel *seen*, *known*, *loved*, and *liked*. I experienced all four of these as a child, and many of the strong families I admire seem to balance these aspects well.

KIDS NEED TO FEEL *SEEN*

"Seeing" your kids is the first step in building a connection. This feels as obvious as saying, "When you give birth, it will hurt." But it truly is important! What I mean here by *seeing* is noticing, observing, and being aware of how the child is *really* doing. The goal is to prevent a situation like my friend Bill told me about years ago that I have never been able to get out of my head. "My brother was basically invisible," he said. Now, I don't think anyone in that family intended to have a kid and forget about them. None of us do. Yet, it often dawns on me: "I have looked at my phone probably thirty times today, and I have not looked at my child's face." I am naturally a self-centered person, and I won't pretend that I have a magical solution for noticing all the people you love on a regular basis. But I do have a few practices that help.

Take a Personal Planning Day

On the macro level, one antidote I have found is a personal planning day. Two times a year (once before school starts, and once in the week before Christmas and New Year's), I have a personal planning day. Among other things, I take time to think about each person with whom I'm in a close relationship. How are they doing? How can I love them better? If you are a kinder person than I am, you probably do this more regularly. But for a selfish and busy person, these semiannual retreats recalibrate me. God will usually give me a "word" (as my charismatic friends would say) for each family member that carries me for a few months and helps me stay focused on their individual needs.

Pray Daily for Your Child

On the micro level, praying daily for our kids can be so helpful. Even if I spend less than a minute in prayer for someone, I get the side benefit of briefly seeing their perspective and worries. Paul E. Miller's "prayer cards," which I mentioned in chapter 5, are an excellent technique for praying specific prayers for your children.[2]

"Collect" Your Child

Another good practice for "seeing" your kids comes from the brilliant book *Hold On to Your Kids*. Gordon Neufeld and Gabor Maté call it "collecting" your kids. They explain, "We have less margin for error than parents ever had before. We face too much competition. To compensate for the cultural chaos of our times, we need to make a habit of collecting our children daily and repeatedly until they are old enough to function as independent beings."[3] How do you collect your kids? The basic idea is that after you've been separated from them, whether from sleep, work, a playdate, or whatever, you "collect" them: you acknowledge them warmly—greet them by name, make eye contact, ask how their time went while touching them (even the older grumpy ones who may not seem to like touch!), and let them know they belong to you and you care about them.[4] It's a small, simple thing that is so important. Since reading that book, I love observing this practice "in the wild." I'll see a friend picking up her kids and note how she smiles, makes eye contact, reaches for her children, and greets them. It's a simple ritual that keeps kids close throughout life's comings and goings.

Be Aware of How Your Child Is Really *Doing*

Beyond greeting our kids, we need to have our finger on the pulse of how they are *really* doing in general. When I was in eighth grade, my mom said to me at bedtime, "Where is my happy, smiling Jessica? I miss her. Where did she go?" I didn't realize I was that transparent. What was wrong was that the boy I was interested in liked my cousin. I am sure that I did not articulate that to my mom. But somehow, I must have said enough, because she said, "You know, some people are like fireworks. They're big and loud and make a display. Other people are like candles. They are bright and steady and keep lighting the room. You are a candle, Jessie." This was thirty years ago, and I can still hear her voice saying these words. She *saw* me.

This can be hard, as sometimes we are seeing the trees but not the forest. When you spend every waking minute with someone, you miss things. Big things, sometimes. It's here I think community and context are so important. Do you have people in your life who love your kids *and who you listen to*, especially as it pertains to parenting wisdom? It is hard and painful to listen to people tell you things about your parenting, your kids. But wounds from a friend can be trusted. One time my sister told me, "You worry a lot about one kid and never worry about the other kids." That hurt. It also helped.

KIDS NEED TO FEEL *KNOWN*

In the beginning, it feels like your kids are a part of you. (Because they *are*, in the beginning.) Slowly, their own personalities begin to take shape. Gradually any illusion of control you may have had fades; they are their own little people! It can be exciting and terrifying to see their personalities develop. Knowing each member of the family means opening your eyes to the strengths, struggles, and quirks of these wonderful beings.

Let's talk first about the good things. Do you verbalize all the traits that are wonderful about your family members? I probably comment on a child's strengths one time for every one hundred times I think about them. I am really bad at this. Chuck Swindoll notes, "Members of a healthy family express affirmation and encouragement often. . . . You are not born with a well-defined sense of self; you discover yourself through the influence of those important to you." Swindoll distinguishes between encouragement and affirmation: encouragement relates to what you *do*, while affirmation relates to who you *are*.[5] It has always bothered me when parents verbalize negative things about their children *in front of* their children. We become what is spoken over us. Speak life!

It's also wonderful when someone sees the little quirks and idiosyncrasies that make us *us*. Recently a friend said, "Well, we all know Jessica wouldn't miss a meal!" I felt weirdly loved. I created the *Family Question Book* with 250 questions that help us to do just this—to learn about and affirm those little things that make us each unique.[6] It's like the games we used to play back in the prairie days when we had no cell phones on road trips. It's easier with some family members than with others. My mom frequently referenced the "conversation pie," pointing out that certain members of the family were eating way more than their share. You may have to work harder to get to know some members. I say all this because it won't necessarily feel like All-Star Mothering to smile and say to a child, "Is sitting on top of the heating vent with your blanket your favorite thing in the morning?" But watch what happens. It's impacting your child, because it feels good to be known.

And alas. Also the bad things. Do you have a family culture in which you can discuss weaknesses and sins in a healthy way? I'll tell you what is one of the most reassuring things in my life: I can walk into a room with my brothers-in-law, my parents, and even a teenage nephew or two and say something like "Well, today I think I'm dying of a parasite in my nasal cavity." (I wish I could say this was never a thought I had . . . but alas . . .) And everyone can laugh with me. I am not proud of my hypochondria, but it really helps to have people who know this thing about me. Sometimes they don't laugh, though. They tell me I need to see a counselor. I really think this is one of the most magical things about my family—the ability to speak of personal struggle, sometimes with a touch of well-placed humor, sometimes with the soberness it deserves. What would it look like to establish this kind of culture as our children grow up? More on this in chapter 13, but for now, seek to normalize talking about the Stuff Everyone Knows Anyway. When it's couched in an environment of grace and unconditional love, speaking freely about our sins and weaknesses can be a life-giving thing.

KIDS NEED TO FEEL *LOVED*

And of course, at the root is love. I remember my pastor saying during our premarital counseling session, "I have the same certainty that the sun will rise as that my wife will love me." What a powerful thing to say. May God grant us this type of "Never Stopping, Never Giving Up, Unbreaking, Always and Forever Love"—the same type of love He shows us.[7]

I am going to take a stab in the dark and say that you love your kids. You are such a good mom that you are willingly spending your time with this book, learning how to love them EVEN MORE! Way to go, you. So of course we love our kids. The question is, how do we make them *feel* it? Furthermore, how do you do this when you as the mom are, to quote Bilbo Baggins, "stretched . . . like butter that has been scraped over too much bread"?[8]

This requires some real strategy. You may have heard of Gary

Chapman's description of the five love languages: words of affirmation, quality time, physical touch, acts of service, and receiving gifts.[9] It is helpful to understand these. See the sidebar for a few other love languages I have come up with in our fifteen years of parenting.

Unique and Particular Love Languages

- Unexpected waffles
- A clean toilet
- A new piece of furniture
- Napkin lunch box letters
- A treat after a doctor's appointment
- Homemade brownies for an after-practice treat
- Putting down the phone
- Mending a stuffed animal
- Watching someone's "cool trick"
- Letting someone choose the music
- Buying a special snack "just because"
- Taking someone with you "just because"
- Letting someone open an Amazon package
- Getting someone out of school early to spend time with you
- Letting someone skip school to hang out with you for no good reason
- Going to see a fort even though you are in the middle of making chili
- Admiring a LEGO creation with your whole heart
- Playing Sequence even though your brain is fried
- Listening to someone retell a dream that is so long, you will need a bathroom break
- Staying next to someone's bed for a few seconds after prayers are over

Thinking about the unique ways we can express love is a good reminder of a few things:

- Be encouraged—while Motherhood is epically hard work, NOT ALL OF IT has to be epically hard. Sometimes it is the little things, the unexpected things, that make a big difference.
- Don't forget to notice things. Who loves what?
- Don't be afraid to let your kids love you back. Nothing wrong at all with dropping hints about what Mother's Day breakfast you'd like, asking someone to reheat your cup of coffee, or giving subtle ideas for Christmas presents ("What I'd really love more than anything is a bookmark! I wonder if someone would make me one!"). When your kids bless you, smile and act super grateful. *Their* gifts of service and love are just as important as yours in building bonds between the two of you.
- Ask your kids (and husband?): "What's the nicest thing I've ever done for you?" I bet you'll be surprised at the answers.

Loving a Child Through Their Struggles

When I think about connection, the picture that immediately comes into my head is a happy, positive one: a mom and a child, smiling, at a restaurant eating pancakes on a Saturday morning. To be clear, pancake breakfast dates are VERY important to bonding, especially if one of the members involved is a preteen boy whose love language is literally "syrup." However, there are other prime opportunities to connect with a child that you might miss because they seem at first glance to be really un-fun. What I am talking about is when your child is struggling to learn a skill or a character trait.

Let's go ahead and state the obvious: it is not fun when your child is struggling. One, you hate seeing them struggle for their own sake. Two, you feel responsible, or at least like you need to fix the problem. Three, you have no idea exactly how to fix it. Weighed down by this vague blob of yucky feelings, you feel more like avoiding the situation. However! This is a ripe opportunity to connect with your child. If you play your cards right, this icky struggle might accomplish more than a pancake breakfast ever could.

God made us parents just for these situations, to help a child grow, with His grace. This is the thing that we signed up for. So, like the stages of grief, the first step is acceptance that we do actually have to deal with this thing.

And here's the unfortunate kicker. This will not initially feel like fun and bonding for your child either. It will feel terrible to them too. But keep your eye on the goal.

Let's say (in a hypothetical situation) that you have a kid who is struggling with being kind to siblings. (Obviously I don't have personal experience with this, but I'll try my best to relate. Ha.) Here is what connection could look like. First, you notice the struggle and don't ignore it. You spend a day or two praying about it. (You could skip this step, but expect to make a lot of apologies if you do.) After you pray, God will give you new insight. How do I know this? Because He says in His Word, "If any of you lacks wisdom, you should ask God, who gives generously to all without finding fault, and it will be given to you."[10] I have prayed that verse back to God many times. He has always shown up. I can't predict what God might impress upon you, but I have seen some common themes when I have asked God for wisdom for an unkind child. God usually tells me to get my grumpy child away somewhere and love on them. He might nudge me about questions to ask to get at what's behind the meanness. And He reminds me that love without consequences or boundaries isn't really love. So I restate the goal to my child, pointing to God as the ultimate rule-giver:

"Love is patient, love is kind."[11] Then I set up clear consequences. We work together through the messiness and will probably repeat the process a dozen times over the next few years. (The long game, remember?)

Let's say, in a different scenario, you have a child who is suffering from the consequences of being disorganized. Even though it might seem more fun (nay, more loving!) to go out shopping and for donuts, I propose that sometimes to love the child, you have to deal with the room that looks like it threw up on itself. Sometimes loving is executive skills training. Sometimes it means you spend the morning together getting rid of all the JUNK this child has managed to sneak upstairs. Your goal is not merely to dispose of the "special" rocks and leaves (why, oh, why??) but also to instill organizational skills at the same time. Maybe you make a chart of how to clean the room daily. Maybe you talk through the process of "keep, save, give away." The point is, you are seeing and knowing that child. You are not leaving them in their mess, literally or figuratively. You are loving them enough to train them. Sometimes bonding is pancakes, and sometimes it is a clean and organized book bag after an afternoon of tears. Parenting is like that.

Love Is Not Love Without Discipline

I want to say a little bit about discipline. We may often feel that discipline is contrary to love. It doesn't feel very loving, like some of the things we have listed above. I understand and relate to this feeling. But ironically, love is not love without discipline.

My parents loved me enough to not let me sit in my dirty diapers, literally or metaphorically. Don't let your kids stay in their poop. Despite having such wonderful examples, I struggle to embody this myself. I have this internal angst every time one of my children needs to be told no. Instantly I come up with a hundred good reasons why I should let them do what they want.

They've had a hard day. I don't have the energy to deal with the arguing. They deserve it. It's not that big of a deal. We are afraid to discipline because we don't want to be unloving, but ironically, not disciplining is not loving.

But of course, we are human, and we will not always feel super loving toward someone who is generally being annoying and difficult. That's why it's helped me to keep saying to myself, "Love hard, discipline hard." Whatever you do, whatever the cost, discipline with your whole heart, taking seriously the poop that someone is sitting in. Get on your knees when you are perplexed. God will give you insight and wisdom. But then—rather, *and* then, at the same time, love that child with your whole being. Real love. Give the consequence, and also the hug. Give the punishment, and also take them to breakfast. Follow through on the thing you said would happen if their behavior did not change, but also pick up a pack of gum or candy "just because" and put it on their pillow. You are so much smarter than I am about your kid; you know what they would love. When you are most annoyed with them, they need your loving discipline the most.

KIDS NEED TO FEEL *LIKED*

I saved "liked" until last, because I wonder if it is the most important. Of course my parents loved me, but better yet—I knew they *liked* me.

Seen, known, loved, and liked: I can think of at least one season in life when I was doing a bad job of all of these at the same time with a particular kid of mine. At the risk of spoiling the ending, I'll tell you up front that God worked a profound miracle. When I think of this child right now, my heart honestly feels like it will burst with so much love and joy. I look at this child and just feel absolute pride and delight.

The healing began in the hallway outside of my closet, where

I had plopped in utter despair one night in August. "Lord, You have to help. You have to help." My child did begin to change following this prayer, but only after I changed first. God helped me to see several things. First, I realized that this child was waking up each day with two strikes against them: I was holding resentment and treating this child differently from the other two. What must that have been like? Second, I realized that much of my annoyance was due to misunderstanding this child's personality. Don't get me wrong—sins were committed all around. But on my end, I did not understand or relate to this child, and that in itself was causing friction. God sent me the first clue of this at our homeschool co-op one day, when we were all discussing our current most difficult children (like you do). The name burst forth from my mouth, and my friend Abby looked up with a laugh. "Wow! Things are pretty good if that child is your most difficult one!" She said it like it was common knowledge.

That was quite a revelation. Not everyone, apparently, was seeing things the way I was. This was confirmed when I reached out to my mom and mother-in-law for advice. Yes, that is how desperate I was. (Sidenote—I have found grandmother insights typically are worth the discomfort involved in asking.) Both grandmothers had the same response, which had a whiff of something resembling kindness toward my child. It almost felt like they did not see how terrible this child was, because they said things like "That child is not terrible at all." It was quite confusing.

Gradually I began to see beautiful, wonderful things about this child I had not appreciated before. And God filled my heart with so much love and also *like*. The weird thing is that kids who are treated as if they are pleasant start acting pleasant.

There are a million ways to connect with our kids, but there is no substitute for really liking our kids. If you find yourself in a season of not having such warm feelings toward a child, here are some questions you might ask yourself:

1. Is a lot of this situation happening because I failed in my role as authority figure and have allowed unpleasant behaviors to be normalized? (If so, see chapter 3.)
2. How much of this is due to personality differences?
3. When I ask someone who loves my child for their honest opinion, is their take the same as mine?

If you answer these questions honestly, it's quite possible you'll end up outside of your own closet praying your own desperate prayer. Maybe you need to go to that hallway now, so to speak. My experience is that we can't untangle ourselves from this sort of mess, but I have found God to be so faithful in answering my honest prayers.

BONUS: KIDS NEED TO FEEL *NEEDED*

Okay, I have to add one last bonus item. And this is really terrific news for us: *kids need to feel needed*. You need help, and your children need to help! Belonging comes from being needed. Think about it: Have you ever been in a group where your input wasn't valued? How did that make you feel? You probably wanted to escape this commitment as fast as you could.

We often hesitate to give our kids jobs, but the irony is that being truly needed bonds them to the family. Recently I read *Hunt, Gather, Parent: What Ancient Cultures Can Teach Us About the Lost Art of Raising Happy, Helpful Little Humans*. The author observed the Maya culture and was stunned by what she saw: "What *really* stood out was the children's helpfulness. Everywhere I went, I saw kids of all ages eagerly helping their parents."[12] This is quite different from what typically happens in American homes today. What accounts for the difference? Maya culture emphasizes that everybody has a purpose, even toddlers.[13]

The book draws a contrast between a child-centered culture, where family events are scheduled around the children—birthday parties, sports, activities (sound familiar?)—and an adult-centered culture, where children get to pitch in and help with the "real work" of running a household. The author points out that children actually love this work. They love to be valuable. "Every time we give a child an adult task . . . we are telling that child that they are part of something bigger than themselves."[14] I have caught a sniff of this vision here and there as I've implemented some of her ideas. It's contagious, and truly a compelling way to run a family.

GIRLS, BOYS, AND TEENS

Before we close out this chapter, I wanted to share a quick word about connecting through specific scenarios. As I mentioned in chapter 6, anxiety in girls is skyrocketing. If you have a daughter, you should absolutely equip yourself with tools to walk her through anxiety if it arises. The most helpful book I know of is Sissy Goff's *Raising Worry-Free Girls*. The author encourages parents to help their daughter identify when the "Worry Monster" is hovering nearby. (Sidenote: as someone who has anxiety, I've found that distancing myself from the emotion and seeing it as something "outside me" is a giant first step to conquering it.) Goff encourages parents to then help their daughter identify what has triggered her anxiety, to have her move and breathe mindfully, to distract her with a question, and then when she's calm, to go back and talk to her, encouraging her to put words to her emotions.[15] Similarly, years ago I read Rachel Jankovic's *Loving the Little Years*, and her vivid comparison of girls' emotions to wild horses has stuck with me. Rachel says, "We tell our girls that their feelings are like horses—beautiful, spirited

Creative Ways to Connect with Kids Individually

Date night. One mom said her young son "took her on a date," opening the door for her, ordering, and so on. What a cute twist!

Ten minutes of undivided attention. Your kid can redeem it however they want. I have given someone a back scratch, heard a guitar concert, and listened to someone talk for ten straight minutes. Ha.

Monthly "stay up late" nights. Each child gets a late bedtime on the day of the month that corresponds with their birthday. They get to stay up an extra hour and hang out with Mom and Dad!

horses. But they are the riders. . . . The goal is not to cripple the horse, but equip the rider."[16] This gives me language to help my daughter navigate changing emotions.

Now: on raising boys. The cruelest thing I ever heard someone say was "A daughter's a daughter for all of your life; a son's a son until he finds a wife." While painful, it was good to hear this to help mentally prepare myself. It just is a different dynamic when mothers raise girls versus boys. Little boys are the best, and slowly, they break away from you in a different way than daughters tend to do. This is natural and healthy.

I recently read the book *Mother and Son* by Emerson Eggerichs. The premise of this insightful book is that just as men value respect, so too do *young* men, and even boys. When I began to implement some of the author's suggestions, I was amazed at how my relationships with my sons improved. Small things—simply shifting the *way* I said something to convey respect, telling them

I admire their character and maturity—made all the difference in the dynamic between us.

When I think of parenting teenagers, I think of the verse "Be ready in season and out of season."[17] Although I doubt the apostle Paul was thinking of parenting, it sure is true that in the moments you feel *least* equipped or energized to invest in your teens, they suddenly have all of these thoughts and feelings to share. The other evening, I could barely hold my eyes open and was just about to turn off the light when my fifteen-year-old (who had been stone-cold quiet the whole day) popped into my bedroom, chipper and alert. "Mom, can we talk about my power-washing business?" Oh yes. I feel distinctly equipped to discuss marketing for a fledgling small business right now! I gave it my best.

As kids near puberty and the teenage years, there is internal and external pressure to become more peer-oriented. It can be tempting to ride with the current and let kids make their new universe their friends. While friendships are certainly worth prioritizing for teenagers, kids need you to remain attached to them. They need you as the compass, centering them.[18]

In *Hold On to Your Kids* the author tells a powerful story of recapturing the heart of his teenage daughter when she wanted nothing to do with him. He took off work for a week and booked a seaside cottage to win her back. He says,

> She first discovered me as a companion for walks and canoeing. Then came a few smiles; some warmth entered her voice. Finally came the talking and an openness to being hugged. . . . When it came time to leave, neither of us was too eager to go back. . . .
>
> Tasha asked why I had left her in the first place. . . . I realized that she was right. It is the parent's responsibility

> to keep the child close. . . . I had unknowingly and unwittingly let her go before my parenting was done.[19]

Throughout childhood, but especially in the teen years, your voice needs to be the loudest one. Fight for it!

SUMMING IT UP

- Knowing your parents like you as well as love you is priceless.
- Sometimes connection means helping someone in an area in which they're weak.
- Boys crave respect, just like men do.
- We need to fight to stay connected to our kids.

TALKING IT OVER

1. Did you feel connected and "seen" by your parents growing up?
2. Which of your kids do you find it hardest to connect with right now? Why?
3. Of the four aspects of connecting with your child—making sure they are seen, known, loved, and liked—which do you find easiest? Most difficult?

COMING HOME

1. Take five minutes and think about each of your children. How are they doing? What might God be leading you to help them with?
2. The next time you see your kids after being away for a bit, try the method of "collecting" them described in this chapter.
3. Ask your kids (and husband?): "What's the nicest thing I've ever done for you?"

One Family's Story: The Fromkes

We met the Fromkes in church, nearly thirty years ago! My sisters and I babysat for them. I adore their family and know you'll love hearing from Jenn about building a strong family, especially with older kids.

We raised our three kids "sticky." Yes, there was jam on faces occasionally, but they all came away from their childhood with a special brand of stickiness.

We stick to our rhythms. Dinner was sacred—no phones, a devotional afterward. We bent over backward so everyone could be there every night. We shifted dinner to after games or practices, or ate early, in the car. The point was to be together and relate face-to-face.

We stick our noses in. We asked LOTS of questions: where they were going, what they were learning, what they thought, what was going on with their friends. We let them know that they were *known* and undeniably *loved*.

We stick together. Our kids cheered each other on at sports and activities. We taught them to stand up for each other at school and to forgive each other at home. We taught our kids they could always count on family, and they learned how to be there for each other.

As our children prepared to leave home, I focused on the *launch* instead of the *loss*. I offered mini life-skills workshops. It was good one-on-one time. Some examples: laundry (don't judge me!), getting an oil change, grocery shopping, cooking, booking travel, making doctor appointments, and understanding insurance. We also decided as a family what we would do for each child when they graduate from college (such as a car, a new mattress, or one U-Haul move).

Every kid knew what to expect, and we worked hard to keep things even and fair. Now they live in three different states, but they talk to each other regularly. And so far, they all still come home. I like to think it's because we're still sticky—and it's sweet, like jam.

8

MEMORIES

How to Celebrate the Sacred, the Seasonal, and the Special (Without Collapsing from Exhaustion)

The men can talk about the Incarnation . . . but we women are the ones who make it taste like something. . . . "And for my next trick, I will take Athanasius' De Incarnatione *and I will say it with cookies and wrapping paper . . . and colored lights and tablecloths . . . and frantically-last-minute-late-night-Amazon orders and ham—and I will do it in such a way that my four-year-old will really* get it, *and it will send roots deep down into his soul where it will anchor his loves and his loyalties and shape his allegiances well into his nineties."*

REBEKAH MERKLE, *Eve in Exile*

I'm so excited about this chapter. If you've read my earlier book, *Memory-Making Mom*,[1] you know that I am passionate about traditions, adventures, and memory-making! Since writing that book, I continue to meet people with the most interesting traditions, and I continue to think up even more ways to celebrate everything with your family. I have also become interested in celebrating the church liturgical year, and I'm excited to share more about this with you toward the end of this chapter. All of these ideas can help us spend time with our kids and develop those connections that lead to strong family bonds.

One huge tip: so that your brain does not explode, I put the "Most Epic List of Memory-Making Ideas Ever" in appendix 1. There are so many ideas in there! Put a little sticky note in that section, and anytime you're hankering for a new tradition or adventure, be sure to reference it!

WHY ADVENTURES MATTER

Since making memories involves work, I think it's good to remember the *why*. I love talking to people about their families, and when I ask what they remember most fondly about their childhood, nine times out of ten they tell me about some great adventure their family shared. These are the things that really "stick."

One night at dinner I asked my kids on a whim, "Hey, what do you think I should include in this book about strong families?" (And yes . . . I did get to such a point of desperation that I asked my children for help.) My daughter said, "Parents should spend time with their kids and not be gone all the time. They should homeschool and take trips and go on a lot of vacations together." Her older brother said, "She said all the things I was going to say." (Yes, every family has one of these.)

I thought it was interesting that my daughter said homeschool, since there are so many days when I feel like no one is enjoying it at all. It's a good reminder that you can't judge things by the outward tantrums. But back to my point—it was those vacations and adventures that stood out! Edith Schaeffer's words, although written years ago, are deeply relevant for tired moms and dads today: "Something will be suddenly possible one day, and the choice will be between taking the hours to have a memory to add to the all-too-short family years together—or waiting for some other time. There must be some times of choosing memories very consciously or your family museum will be . . . empty."[2]

From my Instagram feed, I would conclude that as parents we do *want* to go on adventures, and our generation has probably done a better job at this than others. My parents never took us to a national park, and we never did Disney. I turned out just fine. But I will say that I loved and vividly remember every trip we did take. Making memories together—whether in big, extravagant ways or through simpler shared experiences—binds the family. It adds spark to a normal, humdrum life, gives us shared stories and adventures, and creates a unique and memorable family culture—all solid proof that these memories are *totally* worth the effort!

DISCLAIMER #1: EXPECT HICCUPS

This isn't news to anyone, but there is nearly always some unexpected stress and effort involved in making a memory. This doesn't mean you're doing it wrong!

My husband and I have a little tradition that we've built over many years. We like to have "discussions" in the most adventurous places we visit. In Colorado, we had hiked a respectable four miles when lunchtime approached. I (most reasonably) suggested that we return to the car. This suggestion was overruled. The view was amazing, but let's just say the last thirty minutes would have been more enjoyable had I packed a meat stick. A few years later, we were hiking the Rockies on a very icy day, using snow spikes and ski poles. After our eight-year-old daughter nearly slid off the mountain for the third time, there was a tense discussion about whether "a really good view" was worth potentially losing one of our children. The kids love reliving the hike and the really good view and also my frantic whines that we were all going to die. I guess I am glad I could provide fodder for a good story. In all of these adventures, there was a moment when life did not feel fun and wonderful. The funny thing is, these hiccups don't detract from our fondness in remembering; they often make the adventure *more* memorable.

DISCLAIMER #2: YOU CAN'T DO IT ALL

I'm going to give you a TON of ideas, lists, and examples. Do not interpret this as a Must-Do Checklist for Parents. My goodness, who could do all the ideas?! No one! If you start feeling a little antsy, maybe it is not the right time of the month to read this. Ha. These ideas should make you feel *excited* about some of the things you could do, not *guilty* about all the things you aren't doing. Just take a deep breath and remember—you are only getting ideas! Some are for now, some are for later, some are for never.

By the way, don't get discouraged and think it's too late. As I say in *Memory-Making Mom*, very few people will be reading this as they are pregnant with their first child. Which is to say, nearly all of us have missed opportunities to implement traditions. If you're like me and you have a child who is fifteen (by some wild, incomprehensible development), then you've likely missed a BUNCH of opportunities. Don't let that stop you. It is never too late to try something! In fact, if you have older kids, how fun would it be to get *them* involved in the starting of new traditions? Let them help choose!

One last note about personalizing this chapter: *play to your strengths*. Unlike my sister Jenny, I could not form a sourdough loaf to look like a bunny if you paid me a million dollars. *However*, I love words, so every year I create a rhyming scavenger hunt for Easter baskets. I am sorry, kids, about the sourdough loaves you've missed out on, but we all do what we do. Mama, don't feel compelled to repeat another person's traditions. But *do* find what fits your abilities and your family—and give it a try!

HOW TO CHOOSE?

There are so many traditions and adventures you could do. How do you decide? One tip I have is to talk with your husband and answer this question together: *What are three values that are important to our family?* Todd and I might say the gospel, nature, and togetherness. One fun thing I have never done is the Elf on the Shelf tradition at Christmas. Looking over our list of values, it makes sense that I wouldn't have prioritized that. What I *would* love to do is take our family to Big Sky, Montana. This would check two boxes. Or, here's another smaller idea: as I mentioned, I want to bring more liturgical celebration to our family life. Giving up something as a family for Lent? That vibes. I'll say it again—you can't do everything. Narrow in on your family's values so you know where to invest your time.

Ready to jump in? I am bursting at the seams! I have organized the memory-making ideas into five sections, and I am really proud that somehow they all start with *s*: scenic, seasonal, silly, sacred, and surprises.

SCENIC MEMORIES

What I mean by "scenic" is the grand experiences and adventures, unique to your family's interests, that will really stick out in your kids' memories. Some are great ideas to use for a "Smartt Family Day" (insert your own last name), or they would make great family vacations. These are things like

- See Hawaii, Alaska, Costa Rica, or the Bahamas
- Visit a national park
- Go on a horseback trail ride
- Tour Washington, DC

Check out the list of scenic activities in appendix 1 for many more ideas. Unless you are independently wealthy and have oodles of free time, you probably won't do all of these with your kids. (Hint: that's all of us!) So we have to be strategic. Here are a few tips as you plan for these epic adventures.

First, make a grand plan. I loved seeing the "age chart" Justin Whitmel Earley pictures in *Habits of the Household*.[3] He maps out the years ahead for his family, noting special milestones in each year. I love the large-view concept of plotting the things you know will happen (someone gets a driver's license) along with the things you hope will happen (we visit the Grand Canyon). Of course, your plan will likely get tweaked and rearranged over the years, and that is okay!

Next, read the room. A friend of mine who is a grandparent said she and her husband tagged along with her son's family as they visited the Grand Canyon. They enjoyed it, but the grandkids were two and four, so their nap schedule was tricky, and a lot of the adventure was lost on them. This is not at all to discourage traveling with little kids, but a reminder to try the right things at the right time. In my family, we are in the "golden years" for travel right now. They're old enough to hike without collapsing and young enough that they don't have full-time jobs. So we are trying to pack a bunch of experiences into this stage.

Be super strategic about bringing friends. I touched on this in chapter 6. Vacations are prime sibling and family bonding time. Think long and hard before inviting others into this time meant for building special memories with your kids.

Adapt for younger children. If you have the gift of little children, grand adventures don't need to actually be that grand! Checking out a new park, going to the pet store to watch the snakes, trying a new ice cream spot, watching the pest control guys wrangle a raccoon out of a neighbor's attic (this happened)—these are all little adventures. See the list of "Little Kid Adventures" for more ideas.

Find budget-friendly options. Perhaps the epic adventures sound awesome to you, but they're unattainable for this financial season of life. Check into discounted or free passes for elementary students. Currently, the National Park Service offers a free annual pass for all fourth graders and their families.[4] Consider a "house swap" with a friend, or check vacation house swap groups on Facebook or elsewhere. My friend Erin Odom, author of *You Can Stay Home with Your Kids!*, says, "Look for adventures where you can use coupons. Great Wolf Lodge, for example, offers awesome deals for homeschool families and others via Groupon. We scored a room at an amazing rate that slept our family of six!"[5] And of course, says Erin, don't forget local adventures like free daytime summer movies, school plays, splash parks, and the good, old-fashioned staycation.[6]

SEASONAL MEMORIES

We are fortunate to have "anchors" in our year that prompt us to celebrate: holidays, changing seasons, and birthdays. There are SO MANY ideas for celebrating these. I wanted to share a few I have loved hearing about. Be sure to check appendix 1 for more!

Christmas

I just learned about the Icelandic tradition of *Jolabokaflod*. It means "Christmas book flood," which sounds like my kind of tradition. Pronounced yo-lah-bow-kah-flowed, this tradition started during World War II, when paper was one of the few things that wasn't rationed.[7] It is often practiced by giving friends and family a book and then spending time reading in each other's company, curled up with a hot drink. I love the idea of incorporating this into the Advent season. It is traditionally celebrated on Christmas Eve, but you could surely pick any old day! You could visit a bookstore as a family and give everyone a budget to buy books for all, some, or one member of the family. A used bookstore could be a more cost-effective option. We also have a "homeschool room" near us that's a favorite destination. For a free option, you could simply reserve books for one another at the library.

Little Kid Adventures

- Summer fun: freeze toys in water in a plastic bin for kids to "excavate."
- Fill the bathtub with stuffed animals instead of water and let kids go "swimming."
- Buy pots and pans from a thrift store and play with mud and water.
- Tour the local airport and watch planes take off.
- "Moo" at local cows and see if they moo back.
- Go to the pet store and ask to hold parrots.
- Go to a farm supply store and look at chicks.
- Take a bubble bath with a whole bottle of shampoo.
- Go through the car wash.
- Make a baking soda volcano.
- Watch a parade.

The National Parks in Six Weeks

My friends Katie and Graham took their four kids on a six-week drive to visit the major national parks in the western US. Here's how they did it!

This road trip was years in the making. We started planning and saving seven years prior. We wanted it to be absolutely epic. We planned meticulously, which allowed us to focus on the Lord and serving each other. We delegated parts of the planning to our kids. One selected the hikes and activities. One created organizational systems. Another planned the fun for the evenings. Along the route, we shared what we were learning from God's Word, and we prayed and worshiped together. This trip was a chance to pull away and be rejuvenated by the Lord. It's a trip none of us will ever forget! A few practical tips:

Use an insulated backpack for daily picnic lunches. Saved a ton of money!

Plan meals for the entire trip. Preset grocery lists and find grocery stores in advance in remote areas.

Pack a "kitchen box" with an instant pot, rice cooker, griddle, utensils.

Prep pantry items in one bag per location.

Create a binder with itinerary, shopping lists, packing lists, maps, and passes.

One of my readers gave me this fun tip for opening presents: "A tradition I grew up with is that my mom numbered our presents. We've continued that tradition in our family. Instead of putting names on the gifts, I'll write a number and keep a master list. Then we start youngest to oldest and each gets a chance to guess a number. If they guess correctly and it's a gift for them, they get to open the gift. If they don't, then their turn passes, but if it's been a few turns, we let them have another guess. My kids LOVE this tradition."

Another reader gave me this incredible idea: themed Christmas days! "Since we homeschool, every day during December is a themed day. For example, for Candy Cane Day, I hide candy canes for my son to find (then hide for us), or we play Minute to Win It using the hook of one candy cane to pick up the others. We have science experiments with candy canes, cook with candy canes, and watch a movie. Other themed days include Home Alone, the Grinch, and Narnia (we tried Turkish delight)." I love her creativity! If this feels overwhelming, you could do a "themed Thursday" for the month of December.

You know me and food: I love to hear about what families eat for Christmas dinner. The thing I associate with this meal is a standing rib roast that my mom makes. It is the most amazing meat you could ever put in your mouth. The recipe is some weird thing where you preheat the oven, then turn it off without opening it for six hours. For beloved Christmas dinner traditions, the sky truly is the limit, as long as your family loves it and thinks it's special! Some other ideas to consider: tamales, steak, prime rib or beef tenderloin, goose, Norwegian lefse and meatballs, homemade spaghetti and meatballs, or lasagna.

Finally, I love the idea of keeping a "Christmas journal" to track the activities you've done over the years. You could use any old notebook and put a kid in charge of jotting down what you've

Christmas Eve Traditions

Family sleepover: build a giant blanket fort.

Kid gift exchange: siblings give each other presents on Christmas Eve, when these sometimes-inexpensive gifts are more appreciated and not lost in the shuffle of Christmas morning.

Homemade gift exchange: like a White Elephant exchange but with something you made. Ideas: salsa, a watercolor painting, mancala game, limoncello, body scrub, a wood-burned clock, and a book of beloved quotations.

Foods: We grew up eating appetizers, and I loved it so much. My husband grew up eating shrimp cocktail. I love hearing about other traditions:

- Shepherd's feast (lentils, lamb, dried fruit, goat cheese, Brie and jam, flatbread, dates and figs, grapes, olives)
- Bethlehem-themed dinner with Mediterranean foods
- Chinese, Indian, or Mexican food party
- "Feast of the Seven Fishes"
- Shepherd's pie
- gumbo
- sushi
- bread and soup
- charcuterie
- take-out pizza

done. Keep it with your Christmas decorations, and voilà, you can walk down memory lane when you pull them out every year!

Valentine's Day

So many fun ideas for this day of love! I would start by reading about St. Valentine. His life is shrouded in a bit of mystery, but one book that I would recommend is *Saint Valentine* by Ann Tompert. A clever idea for celebrating the season involves reusing those beautiful family photo Christmas cards. My friend Emily created a Valentine's garland by cutting out the family pictures in the shape of hearts and looping them onto a ribbon to hang on her fireplace mantel.

One of my readers said, "My daughters make paper plate animals that they hang from their bedroom door for the week before Valentine's Day. They cut one paper plate in half and staple a half plate to a whole plate, so it makes a pocket—or the mouth for an animal. Then they decorate them as flamingos or lions or red pandas. Every morning for seven days, I put a small treat inside. They LOVE this!" Another mom said, "Each of my kids makes a Tub of Love: a plastic shoebox decorated with their name and stickers. It gets reused each year, similar to an Easter basket. Also for the first fourteen days of February, I add a heart on their door each morning with a note about something that I love about them. I've gotten them involved too: they take a turn doing a day for one another. It's fun to watch the hearts increase on their doors and see how much they love reading them each morning."

Finally, our family does "Valentine's Secret Santa." You can probably come up with a more clever name, but this is what we call it. The week before Valentine's Day, we each draw a name. Then we do secret acts of kindness for that person all week. On Valentine's Day we give our person a special treat. This has been a giant hit, and it's like Cupid sprinkles Happy Love Dust all over the house. It truly does make you cheerful if you are looking for secret ways to bless someone!

Birthdays

Looking for some fun ways to recognize birthdays? Here are a few ideas, and don't forget to check appendix 1 for more.

I love the idea of landmarking one or two significant birthdays. My friend Cliff took his son to London to watch a major soccer game for his twelfth birthday. In an Instagram post, Cliff said, "It was expensive. . . . Saving is important but making memories is priceless. . . . Watching him see the world for the first time was an inspiring and worshipful experience."

Listen to this super-fun idea from a reader: "A friend I used to work with does Disney, just for the day, with her kids for birthdays. They are on the first plane out, do all the Disney things, and then catch the last flight home! It looks and sounds so fun when I see her posts!"

Of course, not all birthday traditions have to be so epic. I love the simple idea of putting sticky notes around the house with the person's age on them. I bet this is one of those things that is way more fun than it sounds. Similarly, you could put pictures from the child's past year all around the house. I don't print nearly enough pictures, so I'm going to try this. One more idea that has a big return for the effort . . . no school on your birthday!

And I have to mention—what about celebrating your children's spiritual birthdays as well, noting the date that they were baptized, received their first communion, or committed their lives to Jesus?

SILLY MEMORIES

I love the idea of memories "just because." One of my readers said she likes to have a "Yes Day." Stacey shares, "I give my child a list of free or inexpensive ideas. He chooses several, and we write them in an order that makes sense. Some examples: make crepes or find a restaurant that makes them. Go to the movies. Go to the bookstore to sit and read books or graphic novels. Maybe buy a book or two. Convenience store snack run. Trampoline park. Pizza for dinner while watching movies on a mattress in the living room, with the movie projected like an indoor drive-in." The whole "yes day" thing makes me a little nervous, but maybe someday I'll try it. Ha!

Groundhog Day

What? Groundhog Day? Stick with me. Cathy's story is a cool example of making something small into something memorable. I love her effort, creativity, and humor!

We celebrate Groundhog Day very big. . . . I ordered a poster that I thought was small, and it ended up being five feet tall . . . so we went with it. My husband's name is Phil, and I found a groundhog shirt that says, "Just another girl who loves Phil." So now it's a big deal! I have a groundhog cookie cutter, so lunch is groundhog grilled cheese. Breakfast is pancakes in the shape of groundhog faces, and dinner is a meat loaf in the shape of a groundhog face. We have black foam noses that I added white cardstock teeth to, and my daughters and I put our hair up in "space buns" like groundhog ears. Since we homeschool, we have made a salad for the groundhogs near a park (oats and beans in a lettuce-leaf cup), and the kids have made posters of groundhog burrows. Of course, we also watch Punxsutawney Phil and make our predictions!

Another mama has an annual "Splash Day." She shares, "We tell our son's neighborhood friends when it'll be, and everyone brings a bunch of water balloons. They arrive in their bathing suits, ready for fun. We play a few water balloon games, like volleyball and baseball, shoot water balloons with a giant slingshot, and then have the ultimate water balloon fight."

In our home, we celebrate with great fanfare "National Middle Child Day," which is August 12. Well, some of us celebrate with fanfare. Some of us are maybe a teeny bit jealous. But that is okay! We let my middle child pick the food and the game for just a minute of fame and glory.

SACRED MEMORIES

As I mentioned, I have been trying to become more intentional about celebrating the church liturgical year as a family. Truthfully, I have just recently come to appreciate the richness in the many feasts and celebrations. I'm only touching the tip of the iceberg, and it can feel a bit complicated to learn. But as Danielle Hitchen points out in *Sacred Seasons*, "The church calendar is a spiritual discipline."[8] When we honor, remember, and celebrate the seasons and holy days of the church year, we are showing discipline, and just as with other spiritual disciplines, there are tremendous blessings. It's countercultural for us to think about celebrating not only when we feel like it or when it fits with our schedule or our family's mood, but to intentionally commemorate these times as they come up throughout the year.

In case you are not familiar with the church calendar year, I want to give a brief overview. These terms and divisions can differ slightly depending on whether you follow the Catholic, Anglican, or Lutheran calendar, but in general, the seasons in liturgical Western Christianity are Advent, Christmas, Ordinary Time (time after Epiphany), Lent, Easter, and Ordinary Time (time after Pentecost). Here are a few ideas of how you could note these changing seasons as a family.

Advent and Christmas

Advent actually starts the liturgical church year, even though it feels like it ends our year. Celebrating liturgically could look quite different from what we typically do in America. Here's the way people usually celebrate the season: As soon as Thanksgiving is over, hurry up and set up the tree. Cram a bunch of stuff into December. Have Christmas. Take the tree down. Be exhausted.

Now, I'm not intending to slog anyone with guilt. But I have recently gotten a picture of what this season *could* look like. It is actually a deep relief. Here's how it could go: Slowly start Advent the Sunday after Thanksgiving. Maybe decorate your tree in stages, a little every Sunday evening. Maybe put out the Nativity set in stages. Focus on resting, waiting. Finish your decorating Christmas Eve. Then, feast and enjoy the Christmas season, which lasts twelve days—until Epiphany on January 6!

Advent should be a season of waiting. A quiet season. A somber one. No rush. Danielle Hitchen says,

> Advent is a space to remember that longing for the Messiah isn't just a nice thing we say we do. It's the correct response to the genuine horror we should feel when we observe the devastating effects of sin in the world. . . .
>
> It is extremely difficult to extricate yourself and your family from the Christmas mania happening during Advent. But the sacred rhythms of the church invite us to step away from the hysteria and into a holy wilderness. . . .
>
> Make your home a haven from the holiday hysteria.[9]

If we've truly been quiet, waiting, longing, then the dawn of the Christmas season will be a welcome relief, truly a feast and merriment! Danielle rightly points out that this season of feasting can actually be hard! "Sitting in abundance and rest when you're ready to move on is challenging! There will be years when you'll be tempted to end Christmastide feasting early . . . and get back to normal life. Honor the time the Lord has given you to celebrate."[10] How? Take off work for all those days. Use them to do Christmas celebrating. Spread the gifts over the twelve days of Christmas. For more ideas, see the "Twelve Days of Christmas Activities" list.

Twelve Days of Christmas Activities

My sister Jenny has celebrated the twelve days of Christmas for the past few years. Here are some of their favorite activities from December 25 to January 5.

- Bake cookies for a neighbor.
- Get a gift: a new family game.
- Get a gift: a new book for each person.
- Write thank-you cards for Christmas gifts.
- Pick a family gift for our Compassion child.
- Go see a local Christmas light display.
- Watch or listen to *A Christmas Carol*.
- Listen to Andrew Peterson's *Behold the Lamb of God*.
- Read a Christmas book each night with Advent candles burning.
- Sip hot chocolate by the fire while reading the Christmas story from the Bible.
- Bake and decorate sugar cookies and gingerbread cookies to share with others.
- Secret Santa game: each day, draw a family member's name and go out of your way to be helpful to them.

Epiphany, Lent, and Easter

Epiphany runs from January 6 until Lent begins. One way to view Epiphany is as a time of growth in wisdom and favor with God and man.[11] This is a wonderful season for renewing the disciplines together. You could go through a Bible reading plan as a family. Lent is usually observed for about forty days, though this varies depending on which tradition you observe. You may have heard of "Fat Tuesday," where people would eat pancakes or something sweet before beginning their fast. But there is no fasting on Sundays. Sundays are for feasting! Danielle Hitchen suggests that we could give up something other than food during this

Lent season.[12] Perhaps "Fat Tuesday" and Sundays look like movie nights, and no TV on the other days? Perhaps those are the only days you're on social media? There are lots of ways to implement the spirit of quieting our hearts during this season.

Then after this time of fasting and sacrifice, we feast on Easter, of course, to celebrate the Resurrection.

Saint Days

Another aspect of celebrating the liturgical year is noting saints' days and recognizing people who have exceptionally stood up for their faith throughout history, setting an example for us to remember and follow. One we've enjoyed celebrating recently is St. Lucia (or St. Lucy) Day on December 13. St. Lucia was one of the earliest Christian martyrs. This day is often celebrated by having the oldest daughter bring a baked breakfast in bed to the other family members.

When we think of St. Patrick's Day, we might think of beef stew, wearing green, and shamrocks. But St. Patrick was an incredible figure in our faith. I love the idea of reading "St. Patrick's Breastplate," a simple and beautiful prayer, together as a family. The book *The Incredible Saint Patrick* by Jennifer S. Goines highlights his deep faith in a way that will inspire children and adults.

If you're not a giant Halloween fan, consider celebrating All Saints' Day instead. (Our word "Halloween" comes from "All Hallowed Eve," the original name for the night before All Saints' Day.) You can celebrate with a giant fall feast and read about some of the heroic figures of our faith. Phylicia Masonheimer says, "Celebrating All Saints Day connects our family to church history in a very meaningful way, giving us a set time each year to meditate on the strength of our Christian forefathers and what they teach us about life today. It also gives our kids something to focus on and look forward to without replicating the aspects of Halloween that we don't agree with."[13] If you'd like to learn more about saints of our faith, a wonderful resource is the family devotional *A Saint a Day* by Meredith Hinds.

SURPRISES

One remaining parenting goal for me is to give my kids some sort of big surprise. When I was in fourth grade, my sister and I walked out of Red Lion Christian Academy to see my Nana and Pop-Pop standing in front of their giant motor home, waving and grinning. It brings a smile to my face right now to think about it. We headed into the motor home, where we found all of our stuff packed up for the weekend. We felt like celebrities gliding out of that school parking lot in a giant Winnebago. The funny thing is, I really do not remember much about the weekend, and what I do remember is, well . . . a bit of a mixed bag. The grill wouldn't work, it was really hot, there were bugs, and Nana and Pop-Pop got into a little tiff. Regardless, it was the most incredible surprise eleven-year-old me had ever experienced, and that puts a shimmer on the whole memory. I treasure it! I've rounded up a few other stories of surprises in case you, too, want some inspiration.

When my friend's daughter was ten, her dad picked her up from school early one day. Her bags were packed, and she had no idea where they were going until the plane landed in New York City! She enjoyed a few days with just Dad, which included a Broadway show and dinner out on the town. As her siblings approach their tenth birthdays, they're eagerly anticipating their own surprise Daddy trips!

One family drove their kids to their cousins' house, where they did a scavenger hunt for Disney puzzle pieces. The cousins had to work together to find out where they were going. You guessed it . . . that magical place.

One reader told me she packed her kids in the car with picnic lunches. At every stoplight or stop sign, they rolled dice to determine which way to turn until they found a good spot for their picnic!

Another friend said, "The most epic surprise ever was the news about me being pregnant with our youngest. We wrote our kids a letter 'from the baby' and wrapped it as a Christmas gift. Our oldest daughter read the letter out loud. She could barely make it through before bursting into (happy) tears and then proceeding to cry for two more hours!"

Here's one more reader comment, because I know you're thinking about it . . . "I literally got our kids a puppy for the memory of giving them a puppy. Since that day, I've cared for the puppy!" Mama, take note.

DO IT TIRED

A final word about memory-making. A friend in my writing group shared a word of encouragement about writing that I felt was a parallel to mom life. She said that when she looked back over her book, she couldn't tell the difference between the sections that were easy to write and the ones that took gobs of effort. This was encouraging to me—and true; some paragraphs simply breeze out of my fingertips, effortlessly. But others I write slowly, slogging through the recesses of my brain to pull out something worth saying. And now, guess what! I am pretty stinking proud of the whole thing.

Similarly, when I look back on the memories I have made with our family, there were some that came easily, that happened when I was well-rested, emotionally stable, and loving life as a mother. Then there were some when I had to drag myself along. Maybe I was in despair about some mental or emotional hardship, or I was so tired I couldn't hold my eyes open. But when I look back, in a gift of God's grace, they all have the same wonderful hue over them. I'm so glad I made those memories. My kids couldn't tell the difference.

A trendy phrase right now is "Do it scared." I am not sure what the "it" is they want us to do, but nevertheless they are encouraging us to power through the negative feelings. As far as Target mug wisdom goes, it's pretty sound. Don't listen to your feelings; do the thing. Do it tired. Or do it depressed. Or do it lonely. Or do it with period cramps, or after a bad night of sleep. When you look back, you will remember the memory and (probably) not the other stuff.

SUMMING IT UP

- Memories are work, but worth it.
- Observing the church liturgical calendar is a spiritual discipline and also a wonderful gift to us and our families.
- Sometimes the simple and even silly traditions stick with our kids for the long haul!

TALKING IT OVER

1. If you could do one "epic" adventure with your kids, what would it be?
2. Which kinds of traditions are most life-giving to you? Least?
3. Do you have a favorite childhood memory of a family tradition?

COMING HOME

1. Ask your kids if they have a favorite family tradition. You might be surprised about what they love most!
2. Brainstorm with your husband three of your core family values. Use these to decide which memories are worth pursuing for your family.

3. Using Justin Earley's tip in *Habits of the Household*, map out the next few decades for your family, noting big milestones and when you might plan some of your "big adventures."
4. Plan a ____________ Family Day (insert your last name). Only your family attends. Do something all members will love and that you have not done together before. Eat really good food. In the past we've: rented a boat or camper, visited the epic Biltmore mansion, hiked a small mountain, visited a tiger zoo, jumped into a rock quarry swimming hole, and kayaked.

One Family's Story: The Haggans

Paul and Laura Haggan are my sister's in-laws. We have gotten to know them well throughout the years, and I love that they have so many wonderful traditions. They have six kids and many grandkids.

We were both blessed with great families. I'm still close to my cousins. We were given something special, and we kept it going. We were intentional about raising our kids. With six of them, we had to limit activities; they each got one activity and then youth group. We had family dinner almost every night. We always had an open-door policy. We wanted our kids' friends to feel like they were always welcome in our home. One amazing tradition was Friday pizza night with our neighbors whose kids were similar ages to ours. We wanted our kids to hear someone else saying the same things we were saying. We wanted them to be able to discuss issues, rather than just hear us say this is the way it is. We wanted to teach them how to think.

One thing we always prioritize is our weeklong vacation to the beach with our kids and our extended family. We have many shared traditions during this week. Most surround food! Everyone bakes and brings treats from home, and we also bake sourdough bread together. We buy some special snacks that only appear on beach weeks. The kids eat ice cream every night. They also get Tootsie Roll Pops on the beach in memory of Laura's mom who always gave them out.

We make teams on the first day for planning, cooking, and cleaning up. Everyone, young and old, has a job. One night a team is responsible for dinner, another night they are responsible to clean up, and the next night they are off. Repeat. We mix up the teams each year so adults and kids get intentional time together. Pops handles all breakfasts, and we also have a seafood boil night.

We make it a goal to not get back in the car the entire time. Aunt Alison takes the kids for evening rides on skateboards or Rollerblades.

Aunt Julie takes the early risers out to see the sunrise on the beach. Uncle Andrew builds sandcastles with everyone. Uncle John always reads the kids *The Island of the Skog*, *Cyrus the Unsinkable Sea Serpent*, and *Tikki Tikki Tembo*. We play bocce, Frisbee, football, soccer, and kubb, and we have workout challenges. We do a church service on Sunday.

We arrive early and take advantage of public beach access so we can have a full beach day before we even check in to the house. We do the same on the final day after checkout to make the trip two days longer.

9

NEST

Making Home a Place Your Family Loves

The home clearly matters, and matters a lot. And why is that? The home is the beating heart that powers everything else. The home nurtures, feeds, provides rest, gives shelter, and creates a loyalty to itself that is one of the strongest and most compelling of all human emotions.

REBEKAH MERKLE, *Eve in Exile*

The subject of "home management" is difficult to write about. I write this not as a seasoned expert whose house has been featured in *Southern Home* for its neutral-style plantation decor and brilliant organizing solutions. I am just a normal mom with a normal house. This week was VBS week at church. We arrived home yesterday to a homemaking disaster. I could describe it all, but that would probably make your heart rate rise, and I don't want to do that to you.

When a person walks in the door to a home that is a mess, it does something to that person's body. I personally feel really, really tired. This week I legitimately *was* tired, not having slept well. All I wanted to do was ignore the disaster and lie down for a minute. I faced the internal back-and-forth: *Should I rest? Or should I clean?* And/or, *Should I make my kids clean?*

Maybe some of those feelings resonate with you: overwhelm,

dissatisfaction with your space, brain fog with how to fix it, conflicting feelings about what to make your kids do to help. Even though the subject of homemaking—of creating a "nest" for our families—can be a tricky one, I've included this chapter for several reasons.

First, at the risk of being painfully obvious: if you want your family to "come on home," then home needs to be a place where they want to be. There is a bit of a relief in that, though. Not *everyone* has to love your home, as long as *your family* does.

Second, home management is a leading cause of stress in mothers (based on my own extensive field study . . . ha!), and stress in mothers is not conducive to building great family time. Stressed-out moms are not much fun. On the contrary, how do you feel when you've conquered some domestic pursuit? There is a legit mental and emotional burst, isn't there? I am picturing my friends as they tell me about their small-but-not-really victories: "I cleaned out the entire attic today!" "I sorted last season's clothes!" "I organized the pantry!" Feeling these victories has an overflow effect. We want new mountains to conquer. We feel confident and energized in our parenting and homemaking.

HOMES MATTER TO EVERYONE

In short, homes and spaces really do matter to kids (and adults). It's nice to visit the Tetons or see *The Lion King* on Broadway, but your home, of course, is where you are most often. As I brainstormed for this topic, I considered the opposite extreme: What would be the result if someone did *not* value or care for the home? My friend is a police officer. Some of the homes he and his squad go into are heartbreaking. Imagine being a child in a place where no care is given to the home. Maybe you don't have to imagine; maybe this was your own experience. A home can make people feel safe and loved, or scared and alone. While it's true that some of us are more sensitive to our environments, I would posit that all of us can be profoundly impacted by our spaces, for better or worse.

I have a vivid memory of my middle son when he was about three years old. He was just beginning to talk, and he used his words sparingly. So when he spoke, I listened. (As opposed to the other son, who spoke so. many. words. that even someone with the heart of Mother Teresa would have zoned out eventually.) Anyway, as I was tucking my middle son into bed, he looked up behind him. "On these walls . . . I want pictures on these walls. Big pictures of dump trucks and garbage trucks . . . alllllll along these walls."

How funny that this passing comment would stick with me. It was one of those times that you realize, as Charlotte Mason said, "Children are born persons."[1] I did not—would not—think that this little lover of dump trucks and dirt and storm drains would care about beauty. But as he has grown, I have realized that this all-boy, skinned-knee soccer player cares deeply about his environment. Beauty, softness, decor all matter to him.

Knowing this, I feel a little bit like I failed him in those early years. I have never been a good decorator. Making a space beautiful doesn't come easily to me. I am too frugal to buy items we could really use, but then when I finally do buy them, I want to complete decorating projects in one day, which leads to hasty decisions like clearance-rack rugs that shred apart and aren't the right shade and then I hate them.

Since I struggle in this area, I could relate to a story Mystie Winckler tells in *Simplified Organization* about her own homemaking foibles. When a friend came to visit during Mystie's baby-raising stage, the main bathroom toilet was broken. To Mystie's horror, the friend ended up using her disgusting, unclean master bathroom.[2] Maybe it's just me, but I can so clearly picture the state of my master bathroom in seasons when Life Is Falling Apart. I can feel her horror like it is my own.

I remember my aunt and mom visiting after I had a baby, and my aunt going under the sink to get a new trash bag. The level of grime and sludge and old detergent bottles was unparalleled to any in my former or future homes. I want my aunt to come visit now so I can show her my under-sink and redeem myself. Did you hear that, Aunt Marci?

In that same season of life, a mold remediation rep came to our house, because (you'll never believe this) there was water under our sink, and we were afraid it had seeped through the wood panels. I thought this lady would look at the sink and be done. Oh no. She did a FULL HOUSE INSPECTION. This kind, unsuspecting woman went into every bedroom, looked at every dusty air vent, opened every closet. When you look at me, I appear to be an intelligent, semiorganized person. But by the time this woman had filled out the last line in her dreadful report, I am sure she had serious concerns about my well-being . . . and maybe she should have.

In this day and age, we have been freed to be the "hot mess express." We are constantly told that we do not have to have it all together. No shame here, no ma'am. I see the perks of this trend. I am glad that God and my husband love me at my worst. It turns out, though, that hashtags and trendy sayings on T-shirts cannot actually dissolve the innate desire that we humans have for pride in our work. In the Bible, Paul uses the phrase "a worker who does not need to be ashamed."[3] This phrase has always stuck with me. I like being a worker who is not ashamed. It is a happier way to live. And no matter what the world tells me, I want my home to reflect that, even if it's not always perfect.

ARE YOU RUNNING AWAY FROM HOME?

Even though I know the state of the home matters (to us and our kids), there are times I find myself avoiding it. Running away from home, so to speak. As mad as I got at my parents as a kid, I never had the childhood experience of even so much as threatening to run away from home. I had too much fear, since I was the kid whose heart would dip into my stomach over the momentary distress of ending up in a different aisle than my mom at the grocery. No interest in running away from home here, thank you very much. *However, as a mom, I do sometimes subconsciously let the home turn into a place that I would rather not be.* I believe "avoidance" is the psychological word for it. "I don't want to be stressed out by the dishes, so we will go to the park." "We have no routine, so I'll just enroll everyone in camps all summer." That kind of thing.

Important Disclaimer: There are seasons of life when all we can manage is to simply survive. Maybe you have a newborn, are walking through a health crisis, or have just moved, for example. If you're in one of these survival seasons, maybe the best thing for you would be to return to this chapter later.

That said, beware of seasons changing and bad habits remaining. I stopped working out when I had kids who weren't sleeping in the night because I am the kind of person who feels like death on less than eight hours of sleep. Which is fine, but then it was four years later, and I still wasn't working out, because . . . habits. When your margin grows, be sure to turn your heart back to your home. Sometimes it feels super discouraging to even think about homemaking because people live in our homes and make messes, and this isn't going to change anytime soon. Don't feel bad about the messes being made! If you, like me, are a mother doing Good Gospel Things you should be doing, like letting kids play with Play-Doh, making smoothies, reading to your children, prioritizing people over things, having children who wear shoes, and generally BEING A BUSY HUMAN, then your house probably looks like it. At any given point, there are things unintentionally fermenting in the back of your fridge, dust bunnies on top shelves, and muffin crumbs under sofa cushions. There is a 90 percent chance someone's bed is unmade right now, despite the chore chart that says otherwise. It is quite likely there is at least one piece of furniture (but probably twenty) that irks you because it needs an upgrade or isn't the right size or shape or color for where you have smooshed it. But you're dealing. All of this is simply a sign that Real Life is happening.

Homes are places where people poop and stain shirts and cut up snips of paper for inexplicable reasons, never minding to sweep up the remains. They say that your house won't be clean again until your kids move out, and then you'll miss the messes and look back fondly on them. Some days I am not sure.

Nevertheless, we do not just give up. It would be really sad if a wife said, "Well, I will never look like I did when we got married, so why try?" Last month I showed my kids a picture of my husband and me on our wedding day. "Wow," they said. "Dad looks the same." (Awkward silence. Nothing more.) Young, tan, and fit Jessica really had no idea how she should have treasured those days in her heart. Regardless, I keep going! I do what other self-respecting forty-something women do: shut my eyes to the ideal and keep lifting weights and highlighting the grays when I can.

Same thing in the home. What is the home equivalent of letting go of the wedding day glamour but still faithfully caring about your appearance? What does healthy, balanced homemaking look like? The kind that doesn't forbid people from sitting on the sofas or from learning to make ~~pancakes~~ giant messes in the kitchen but also doesn't get discouraged in seeking beauty and order? Striking this balance is our goal.

THE REAL POINT OF HOMEMAKING

I want to clarify the goal of making a beautiful little "nest" for our families (it may not be what you're thinking!). Then we will walk through four arenas in which we might improve our homes in life-giving ways. To state it plainly, my goal here is not to set out some sort of ideal home decorating standard that we all need to reach. There are two questions to ask yourself, and two alone.

Question 1: Is your home a place you like to be?
Question 2: Is your home a place your family likes to be?

Because after all, this isn't a homemaking book. This is a family book. How do we make our homes into places that love our families and vice versa? While your ideal home looks different from my ideal home and looks different from your neighbor's, it is helpful to remember a few guiding principles, and then to translate them into our own family personalities. Make sure you don't miss the end of this chapter, where I've included a lot of suggestions for each of these! Okay, here are the guiding principles: beauty, order, rhythm, and love.

THE VALUE OF BEAUTY

While it is true that each of our homes will be wildly different, a great and happy home will be beautiful. How can I say something so concrete? *Because God invented beauty.* It is a value to Him, and we go against the nature of things by pretending otherwise. This may seem like abstract and flowery language, so let me bring it down to earth with one possible suggestion: *If you have a really ugly, unloved room in your home, when you have the bandwidth, work on making it beautiful.*

Money helps, for sure, but is not necessary. I often say that Ma Ingalls did a fantastic job of building a beautiful home with next to nothing in terms of resources. When you read Laura's description of their primitive cabin, there is an undeniable smack of beauty in the simple wood carvings on the bookshelf, the clean-swept floor, the checkered tablecloth.

Did you like how I said above "when you have the bandwidth"? I am not looking to lay burdens on people who don't have time to brush their teeth. But if you have the margin to do a few things you want to do, then turn your heart back to home and work on that ugly corner that may be dampening your spirits.

I have seen this principle work miracles in my home. A new white tablecloth, some wildflowers on the counter, a freshening up in the mudroom . . . the people in my home notice. When I do something to invest in our home, every single member of the family brightens. I imagine them thinking, *She cares about us. Our family matters.* I know that might sound a bit weird, but see if you, too, notice the change in your family when you invest in your home.

THE VALUE OF ORDER

In addition to beauty, our homes should reflect a sense of order. Again, I take no credit for this wisdom, because I invented none of it. God did! Think about it. He started with chaos and darkness and gave it structure and place. God created a world with symmetry, boundaries, balance, precision, and harmony. It is a good thing when our homes mirror this. What I think is fascinating is that everyone has her own system. My mother-in-law runs a well-organized house. She can grab any random item you need in about two minutes. But her home looks so different from mine! She has a much higher capacity for stuff than I do. She has all kinds of fascinating little knickknacks and decorations. I wonder if she feels that my white home is blank as a prison cell. Order can look different in different homes. But there should be order. Orderliness is a God-given virtue and worth our time.

If you are someone who struggles with order and cleanliness (which, I suspect, is probably 95 percent of us moms), then it's possible that last sentence made you feel icky and depressed. We don't want this. There have been libraries of books written about home organization, so you likely aren't expecting life-changing info here from a mildly organized parenting writer. I just want to say a couple of things for the purpose of this book.

1. Don't give up. It is a long, hard, never-ending fight to wrangle stuff and organize spaces. Every small choice you make toward order (like me forgoing my nap to unpack the VBS tornado) is good work. You are blessing your family.
2. You probably have too much stuff. And you would feel lighter with less stuff.

Maybe a more helpful word for order is "simplicity." I highly recommend Kim John Payne's book *Simplicity Parenting*. Payne says that because our modern life is so stimulating for children's developing brains, we must be intent on creating "islands of calm" for our children.[4]

Well, I may have laughed out loud when I heard this, because "island of calm" does not exactly describe the Smartt household most days. I live a pretty whirlwindy life. I always have a lot going on, more going on than I can handle. I'm sure you can relate! I remember when I was just out of college and living at my parents' house for a brief stint while I was single and teaching English. My mom, I guess, had observed my tornado behavior for a few weeks and said, "Jessica, every once in a while you have to stop and do the maintenance things and take care of stuff." She had thus pinpointed one of the greatest struggles of my adult life. I do not yet have this managed, but my whole family is blessed when I am working toward order in our home. If you need additional resources for managing your own whirlwinds, see appendix 3 for several I have found helpful.

THE VALUE OF RHYTHM

Similarly, we can strive to create predictable rhythms in our home. Again, not my virtue. My husband is the calm and steadying force. (I mean, anyone who can stand calmly in fly-fishing waders, waving a rod for five hours, unbothered to have caught zero fish—that person clearly has much to teach us all in the way of patience.) Once again, this is a virtue that God created. Think about the predictable rhythms and rituals of nature. Our homes function best when they are mini-models of this. Is your home a model of blissfully predictable rituals? Gosh, mine is not. But if God can make the sun rise and set WITHOUT FAIL, despite all the chaos in this world, I guess we, too, could strive to give our families similar comforting rituals.

When I think of consistent rituals in the home that are really life-giving, I think of Corrie ten Boom's father. As Corrie relays in her book *The Hiding Place*, her father spent every morning for fifty years sitting at the kitchen table. He would arrive promptly at 8:30 a.m. and begin reading the Bible aloud to whoever was in the house, no matter what was happening inside or outside the home. Through two World Wars! I don't know about you, but this kind of faithfulness stuns me. I think we just let our lives get too busy.

What rituals do you have in your home? What daily or weekly rhythms mark your seasons? If this is an area you'd like to grow in, I would highly recommend the book *Habits of the Household*. Justin Earley paints a beautiful picture of what some of these rituals could be. I remember the sentence that stopped me in my tracks the first time I read it. "One of the most significant things about any household is what is considered to be normal."[5]

Ugh. That one had me thinking for a while.

Justin continues, "I am suggesting that we reclaim the idea of creating a rule of life in our families so we can produce something other than the typical anxiety-ridden, depression-prone, lonely, confused, and screen-addicted teenager. . . . So we can teach them the peace that comes with knowing the unconditional love of Jesus."[6]

Sign me up!

Of course, creating life-giving rhythms is no quick and easy job. Just like with beauty and order, we are all wired differently in terms of rhythm and structure. Some of us (like my fly-fishing husband) naturally embody this calm, predictable flow that steadies our families. Others of us party animals are thrilled to hop up and go do anything, anytime, whatever the cost. Despite our temperaments, we humans need a certain amount of predictability to thrive.

Look at your people. Are they well-watered and thriving? Do they need more downtime? Are there anchoring rituals in your family life? I don't think any of us would regret an 8:30 a.m. Bible ritual like Casper ten Boom's. Family meals are another sort of calming ritual—although "calming ritual" might seem like a hilariously inaccurate description if you have kids banging sippy cups, chewing with their mouths open, and weeping, like with real tears, over roasted zucchini (this has happened in our home). Regardless, keep faithfully meeting together at the table, with the confidence that it is achieving something in the lives of your kids. Note that rhythms can be weekly as well as daily: the Sabbath dinner, Sunday church, Saturday morning pancakes.

What I am saying is nothing earth-shattering. And yet, doesn't it shatter how most of the earth is living? Culture at large in the West is happily pulling us out of our homes, toward more busyness, away from each other, away from the unassuming regularity of meeting with God and others. On our Sunday drive to church, we pass a soccer field that is—without fail—packed to the max for a soccer tournament. I can't judge, because our family has had its own seasons and weeks of Sunday sports. I guess this is its own sort of ritual. But for what gain? Somehow we are willing to sacrifice so much of our lives for soccer or swim team, but less willing for church or family. Let's prioritize rituals that strengthen our families in ways that truly last.

Here are a few ways to prioritize rhythm in your home today:

- Choose a phrase to say to your kids every evening. Maybe "I love you and I always will." My dad says, "God bless and protect you" when he hugs me before leaving.
- Have a mealtime prayer you say together, or a bedtime liturgy.
- Draft a daily family schedule for the season of life you're in.

THE VALUE OF LOVE

We've talked about the value of beauty, order, and rhythm in our "nests." We've talked about how these things are fleshed out differently in your family versus mine. The last, and possibly most important nest-building virtue is love. As you live out what it looks like for *you* to be the keeper of your home, try asking yourself, "How can I display love in my home? What would bless my family most?" This is empowering—a way to quiet all the noise "out there" and home in on what would be the difference maker within your own four walls.

This is also important because we have all been in beautiful, organized spaces in which we felt clearly unwelcome. Rebekah Merkle says, "You can use beauty to drive people away as well as to draw people in."[7] What is missing? *Love*. You can clean out of love, and you can clean out of anger. (Ask me how I know.) This is just a little reminder that the whole point of this chapter—our whole reason for creating a nest full of beauty, order, and rhythm—is to show love to our families.

YOUR DEEP-BREATH DISCLAIMER

Despite my best efforts, I wonder if you are feeling even more discouraged, stressed, or grumpy about your home. Maybe there are things you have genuinely tried to change in your home or would love to change but simply cannot. I do not want you to end up feeling overwhelmed. Rather, I would love to give you the "permission slip" to pour into your home in a way that is life-giving to you. What would really excite you about your homemaking? What have you been wanting to update, invest in, or learn but have not pursued because you have let yourself become busy with other things? God gave you the gifts and longings He did for a reason. Listen to those longings. Pour yourself into your home.

This is a good time to tell you about my Grammy's house. It wasn't beautiful. It wasn't orderly. It was a cluttered two-bedroom trailer. Because she had an open-door policy and lived on a working farm, there were always people coming in and out, and I think she was never quite sure who would eat the lunch she made. Things felt chaotic.

And yet—*I loved Grammy's home*. It was a "nest" for her family in the truest sense of the word. On a deep level, it embodied Home to me. When I try to figure out why, the only possible explanation is that we were wanted there. We were loved.

SUMMING IT UP

- Home should be a place your family wants to be.
- Homes can look wildly different, but good values to reach toward are beauty, order, rhythm, and love.

TALKING IT OVER

1. Do you ever feel like "running away from home" because it stresses you out?
2. Rebekah Merkle says, "We women could . . . use our position as homemakers to create homes that are utterly compelling."[8] What could that look like for you?

COMING HOME

Use "The Nest Quiz" to discover what each member of your family loves about a home. It might give you some insight into areas you could invest in.

The Nest Quiz

Ask each member of your family these questions to determine what they love about a home.

1. Do you love when your space is organized?
2. Do you love bright colors? What are your favorite colors?
3. What's your favorite room in the house?
4. Which is more important to you: a comfy chair or one that looks nice?
5. If you could add one thing to your bedroom, what would it be?
6. Which do you prefer: lots of decorations or a clean and simple room?
7. Do you like having the same routine each day or doing something different every day?
8. What's your favorite part of every day?

One Family's Story: The Collins Family

I have always been captivated by stories of people making choices to change the trajectory of their lives. That is why I am in awe of my friend Katie Collins. I met Katie at our homeschool community. Katie and Adam have three kids, ages two, ten, and fourteen.

We began our marriage with "normal" goals: careers, a house, travel, and eventually, kids. I went to medical school and then OB-GYN residency. God blessed us with our son while I was in residency and thus started a slow, steady reordering of our goals that we can only see now as His incredible sanctifying work. Leaving my baby to work eighty-plus hours a week was miserable. I felt a deep ache every time I left him. I wondered how long it would take before the pain subsided and I would feel the promised fulfillment from my career.

Three years passed and God blessed us with a daughter. I was now part of a successful private practice, and I had it about as good as it gets: a decent call schedule, workload autonomy, and partners who valued work-life balance. Still, I carried constant guilt, and I agonized over every weekend away, missed school event, missed book and bedtime. I sensed that my kids' childhood was speeding past and most of it was spent in separation.

But God brought us into a church family where we were discipled by couples who valued their faith and their families over other pursuits. The Holy Spirit continued to convict us regarding God's design for our family. It took time to break free. I interpreted my misplaced sense of duty to my career as God's calling for my life. We moved our kids to a Christian school so at least they would learn from a Christian worldview in their many hours away from us each day.

When I was forty-two, God gave us another child. He used her as the catalyst for changing the trajectory of our family. On my short maternity leave, I grieved over sending my older kids away on the bus and over having so little knowledge of what they learned all day. I grieved that it was so novel for them to have their mother home cooking for them. I grieved the family Bible study that we never found time to do. I grieved that I would be leaving yet another infant with someone else to feed and rock and sing to her. Adam came upon me crying and praying for the fortitude to go back to work soon. He said, "Babe, we can sell the house and live differently. You can stop working."

We made plans for me to retire, to take our kids out of school, to learn to homeschool. God has changed our understanding of what is "best" for our kids and our hopes for their futures. We love the time we now have together, preparing food, taking walks, and creating lasting memories as a family.

10

ROOTS

Recipes, Relics, Relatives, and Other Things That Keep Kids Grounded

To be rooted is perhaps the most important and least recognized need of the human soul. It is one of the hardest to define. A human being has roots by virtue of his real, active, and natural participation in the life of a community.

SIMONE WEIL, *The Need for Roots*

My worst subject is science. Physics was my only C in college; darn those laws of motion. My brain hurts when I try to understand anything scientific. I will be honest with you and confess that for this reason, the homeschool science curriculum around here has probably been a bit subpar. I should probably have outsourced science to my plant-obsessed, engineering-minded husband. Unlike me, he finds subjects like horticulture absolutely fascinating. I have learned not to feel insulted if we are on a date and he stops to take pictures . . . of shrubs. However, I'll give it to him; I have recently learned a few things about plants and roots that are downright fascinating. Here are a few fun facts about roots.

- Very often, roots are significantly bigger than the plant. An ordinary four-foot horseradish plant may have roots fourteen feet deep![1]

- Most plant problems (80 percent, to be exact) are caused by root issues.[2]
- Roots can be strong enough to destroy stones, cement, and concrete.
- One root expert noted, "Some of us have always felt the root system is the most important part of the tree—the key to health and longevity."[3]

Interesting, right? Are you seeing the parallels to our reflections on growing strong families? *Strong roots equal health and growth.* Now, what specifically do I mean by "roots" in terms of the family system? Let's look here at the stories, legacies, relationships, and history of our families and how we can leverage these things in building a strong family.

For many people, the idea of family "roots" might evoke feelings of shame, bitterness, disappointment, or grief. Some of us come from strong family systems, and some of us don't. I am not a family psychologist, and navigating complex family trauma is outside the scope of this book. Godly counselors are worth their weight in gold. However, whether you come from a long line of strong, healthy families or from a family tree that is a withering, wilting mess, it is my hope to encourage you in four areas:

- recognizing the power of family stories
- cultivating a deeper appreciation for family treasures
- continuing to form a family identity
- leveraging the support of your extended family

RECOGNIZE THE POWER OF FAMILY STORIES

Telling our kids stories is one of the most powerful things we can do. "This is what stories are for," says Justin Earley, "moving reality from the head to the heart."[4] When we were little, my mom would tell us bedtime stories about "Caroline, Elizabeth, Emily, and Jacob." They'd get in funny scrapes and pickles and eventually learn some lesson that always seemed weirdly applicable to our own lives. Took us an embarrassingly long time to realize those four children were basically the four of us.

I can now appreciate the gumption it took my tired mom to conjure a made-up tale at the end of a long day. I also see why she did it. Stories are more than the sum of their parts and more powerful than we could ever imagine. Of course, not all of us parents have such imaginations. And that is completely okay! Although I'm a writer, my "fiction brain" is sorely underdeveloped. So, I have gotten in the habit of telling my daughter "mini-stories with a lesson" at bedtime, based on memories from my childhood. The "mini" part puts less pressure on me to remember grand, complicated tales, and it is also very convenient because she is one of those children who comes up with any and every excuse to keep you in the room until 11:35 p.m. I even have a "note" on my iPhone for saving ideas for these stories as they come to mind during the day. Some of them are more funny than anything else. A recent one: "My Grammy used to have a dachshund named Darla who loved food. Darla would hear you opening the refrigerator and come running in case she might get a bite. Eventually she ate so much that she got stuck under the couch and couldn't get out. The moral is: don't eat too many desserts." That story really cracked my daughter up.

Even if we can't create wild tales or remember much in the way of stories from our own childhoods, I think it's worth the effort to come up with our own version of storytelling. I've observed two things as I've been telling stories: one, that I remember more things than I thought, and two, that even little memories are satisfying to her. I will really be scraping the bottom of the barrel for memory tidbits and think, *This will not be interesting to her at all*, but somehow, it is. Our kids just want to hear from us. (Particularly when they're little, so let's take advantage!)

Story time does a few things for us as a family. One, it is bonding us; it's a kind of a friendship blooming. Two, it makes our children realize "Mom has felt this too." Kim John Payne reminds us that family stories are hugely important, particularly when a child is getting bumped or bruised by life's circumstances. "There is a feeling of 'We are us.' . . . You come from good people. And here are our stories."[5]

I also want you to know what an act of desperation story time can be. Often I am climbing the stairs, totally exhausted, not a shred of a memory in my mind, and somehow by the time I'm sitting in bed with my daughter, God has given me something to share.

As you're telling your own stories, think back. You might remember tidbits about your parents and your grandparents and even great-grandparents. These are gold. Tell and retell. One resource that I cannot recommend highly enough is Storyworth or similar gift ideas that will provide prompts to help you or your loved ones tell your story and then print it in book form. What a privilege to have their words and stories in writing. My Aunt Jamee did this with my grandmother, just in time before the dementia really kicked in. We now have little notes from my Grammy's life that my children, and their children, will be able to read.

Maybe your family history is tarnished with some dark spots. (Whose isn't?) Maybe there are people you aren't so proud of. Maybe it's complicated. I would still encourage you to share about these ancestors, as age appropriate. No one is one-dimensional. Find details to admire or note. Or share a lesson you've learned from observing their life. Continue to pass on little details about those in your family line. Give your kids something to hold on to.

VALUE FAMILY TREASURES

When Todd and I had been married for about five years, my father-in-law notified us that as Todd was the oldest living Smartt grandson, we were to be receiving "Judge Smartt's chest of drawers." Now, Judge Smartt was evidently a wonderful man, but a relevant piece of information is that his chest of drawers is MASSIVE—*fourteen feet long and ten feet high, to be exact.* The dudes from Two Men and a Truck said it was the largest piece of furniture they had ever moved in their lives. I admit that I was a bit grumpy about this monstrosity taking up half (literally, half) of a room in our house. My gracious in-laws overlooked my forced "enthusiasm" and gushed over how wonderful the piece looked in our now jam-packed dining room.

But fast-forward ten years, and I am so, so grateful to own Judge Smartt's chest of drawers. First of all, it's a gorgeous piece of furniture—like, the most commented-on thing in our house. Second, how cool is it that we have a piece of furniture that nearly dates back to the Civil War?! This cabinet had graced Judge Smartt's Knoxville law office, and then Nanny, Todd's precious grandma, brought it home, wallpapered the back of it, and lined up her dishes in there. Now this piece of history is in our very home and will one day be passed down to our oldest son (and whatever good sport of a wife he eventually finds).

I love IKEA as much as the next girl, but I doubt that my grandson's wife is going to be proudly displaying my Facebook Marketplace steal of a dresser. Some things to think about: Do I have items of value to connect our future family to their past? If I inherit such items, will I value them enough to hold on to some of them, even if they don't "fit" completely with my style? When my Grammy moved in with my mom, I got to keep a few of her dishes. It is an absolute joy to pull out the green, flowered Tiffany china when I have friends over for dinner. What a treasure!

Recently I discovered the show *Milk Street's My Family Recipe*.

The premise is that viewers submit a long-lost recipe, or pieces of one, in the hope that acclaimed chef Christopher Kimball and staff can recreate it. What's so fascinating is that when the viewers taste the recreated "Grandma Margaret's Coconut Cake," something happens on an emotional level. They are filled with fondness for the food, of course, but even more for the person who used to make them this food. These recipes are stories and relics in and of themselves. There are always tears. It was convicting to me, honestly. I doubt anyone is going to be hankering after my gluten-free, refined-sugar-free baked raisin oatmeal recipe in fifty years. It makes me want to work harder on perfecting recipes that are really "us," that have the power to be a reminiscence and a treasured memory. (And also maybe have more sugar. That seemed to be a common theme.) Alas, it's harder with food allergies, which can make it feel as if you're baking with one hand behind your back. Nevertheless, I persevere. If you have recipes that hold special meaning for your family, keep making them! Ask your kids what recipes are "us." Keep telling the stories. And don't be afraid to make new traditions! I might be wrong, but I think one big lie Satan likes to tell mothers is that it's too late. (It's never too late.)

FORM A FAMILY IDENTITY

In addition to retelling stories and valuing heirlooms, growing deep roots as a family looks like using "we" statements to cement your family identity. These can be little things. I recently heard my daughter's friend say, "The Todd family loves eating subs. That's just something we love." It made me smile. Here are some things you might say: "We always play a game on Friday." "We love soccer games." "We don't want to miss waffles on Saturday."

These "we" statements matter particularly at times of discipline. It is a powerful thing to shift from "you" language ("You need to work on this") to "we" language ("We don't speak that way to one another"). Tuck this away to use when you are making a countercultural choice, as well. There is tremendous power in the phrase "We are the Smartts, and we _________." Embrace the different. I do not mind using language like "Well, it's great that another family doesn't clean the shower every week. We are the Smartts, and we do!" Or "I know that that person gets to watch that movie, but in our family, we are going to wait." Build that unit.

Another powerful tool is to build a family mission and values statement. You might do this several times over the years as you find the need to clarify and recalibrate. Sometimes a "family mission statement" can feel like this giant thing, and depending on your personality, it can either make you feel extremely pumped or like you want to take a nap. (Usually there's one of each in every marriage.) Don't let it overwhelm you. God knew your disposition and your gifts, and He chose you to raise your kids. It is important to have a goal, but it doesn't need to be a seventeen-page document that took you months of torturous family meetings to formulate. If crafting a family mission statement is something that excites you, I highly recommend Stephen Covey's book *The 7 Habits of Highly Effective Families*, which outlines this process in depth. Here are the steps in a nutshell:

1. Plan a special family meeting. Make it a celebration! Go away to a hotel for a night, if you can. Or have a pizza party or sundae bar.
2. Ask questions and let everyone contribute. "What's your favorite thing about coming home?" "What makes our family unique?" "What things are important to us?"
3. Based on the answers, create a list of your family's core values. You might include things like integrity, service, beauty, faith, financial stewardship, hospitality, adventure, or industry.

4. Use these values to create a sentence or two about your family. (Examples: "In our family we use our time, money, and talents to glorify God and help others." Or "In our family we love God, open our home to others, and treasure beauty.")
5. Now post your statements where they are visible and refer to them often![6]

You might be wondering what's the ideal age to include your kids in your family mission planning. Truly, I can see the virtue of doing this several times over the course of your family's journey! The first time, if you have kids under ten or so, you as parents will obviously be directing the conversation a bit more. Or perhaps you and your husband would enjoy taking a night to brainstorm, just the two of you, and then having a pizza night to "present" your family vision.

As your kids approach the preteen and teenage years, buy-in is key. I can see this becoming a more collaborative event. Either way, keep it short and upbeat, and include food or something fun.

LEVERAGE YOUR EXTENDED FAMILY STRATEGICALLY

I'll be honest: I've been semi-avoiding this section. I'm typing it now on a plane, and the kid in front of me is playing a video game in which he has to jump around a room and avoid landing on these little land mines. This feels oddly appropriate. Extended family: parents, in-laws, aunts, and uncles . . . what a minefield! What a tricky subject to navigate as an author when you don't know the person who is reading! I don't know your stories, your relatives, your specific concerns, or the trauma potentially associated with your extended family.

And yet, I don't feel this book would be complete without a mention of it. Extended family can be another layer of roots for your family, digging deep into the soil, giving footing, bracing the tree, making it stronger. More family girding you up in life can be a great thing.

As I said, this is a tricky topic because I don't know your history, and I am limited by my own personal experience. Only you and your husband can determine when a relationship is essentially harmful to your family and when boundaries must be put in place. At the same time, I think it's important in this age of "toxic relationships" to also acknowledge that every one of us is a sinful human being and sometimes when you interact with other sinful human beings, you end up with hurt and baggage. We must be careful to avoid dismissing relationships or people simply because they're hard. The future of relationships like this requires great discernment and is well beyond the scope of this book to address. Approach it with much prayer and wisdom. Of course, a wise, godly counselor can help you process issues such as these.

If you happen to have a healthy relationship with your extended family, I'd like to offer some tips to maximize those relationships. Some of this may feel obvious, but I would be remiss not to say it. First of all, if you have healthy family relationships and can feasibly live near family, I urge you to strongly consider it.

Seven years ago, my realtor sister began looking for land on which we could build a big family farm. I hated the idea. I literally prayed it would fall through. One night during our beach week vacation, our family sat down to talk about it. It was highly emotional. We all threw out words we didn't mean. From my perspective, I loved our little neighborhood, and I hate having things change. I eventually left the decision up to my husband. Fortunately, he loves four-wheelers and wide-open spaces, so he said, "We're doing this." And honestly, it's one of the best things that has ever happened to us or our kids. When I get up in the morning, I sit on the front porch and see my daughter and her cousin walking in their overalls to meet my father. The little crew of them will "do the horses" for the next half hour. This is just a snippet of our life—one of many, many gifts that being close has afforded us. (Leftovers has been another. Everyone saves me their leftovers.) I realize that this—moving to be close to family—might be a giant dream that could never happen for some people, even though they might wish it could. If you are considering this change and are able to do it, here is my vote: yes. It's hard at times, but on the whole, it's wonderful.

Of course, our choice means we don't live near my husband's family. If you do live away from family, you can still stay close, if you're intentional about it. His family has done such a wonderful job of staying connected. My mother-in-law is the sweetest at remembering any and every special day with cards and a gift-wrapped package. I think they know her by name at the post office. My sister-in-law Julianne FaceTimes us often, sends drawings and letters regularly, and comes to visit anytime she can. She also *always* remembers birthdays. Todd's family has a saying: "You always get a birthday gift; it just might be months later!" They have encouraged me so much in this area to make the time and space to be involved with those we love and not lapse into the "out of sight, out of mind" mentality that can be so natural.

This is a situation where technology can be our friend. What an age we live in with technology. Why not use this for good to bind your family together? Utilize group texts and video calling. Make your kids sit still and talk. Most children are terrible on the phone at first. Don't be shocked; help them work on this skill. My sister recently found this amazing digital photo frame. Family members can send pictures to an email address belonging to this digital frame . . . which means that the person with the frame can easily enjoy up-to-date pictures of faraway family members. Hello, grandparent gift! If you have parents who are believers, utilize these prayer warriors!

Another way to intentionally bolster extended family relationships is to maximize the family vacation when you are together. Leonard Sax says, "When you are planning a vacation, look for opportunities for your child to connect with her aunts, uncles, and grandparents. You want to give your child a different perspective. You want to connect her to your culture."[7] I've included my friend Natalie's story at the end of this chapter, because I absolutely love her family's tradition of a giant family vacation. Maybe you haven't been blessed to be in a family with a legacy-vacation . . . how cool is it to think that you could be the one to start it! The most annoying thing about vacations is that they are so stinkin' expensive. Yet, I think they are worth budgeting for. One of my favorite memories with Todd's family is the year that we went to Kiawah Island in South Carolina. When the kids went to bed (which was like seven o'clock . . . back in the good old days—ha), we grown-up kids ate ice cream, played cards, and then rode bikes around the island.

My friend Kathy's parents host all their grandkids for "Grandparent Camp." The kids go to VBS at their grandparents' church, and when they age out of VBS, they volunteer. I think that is a wonderful tradition . . . and smart! They have a week of activities planned that they don't have to organize! If you don't live near family, these tradition-trips can be a glue that holds all of you together over the years.

BONUS ROOTS

In case you are one who has not been able to enjoy the gift of extended family relationships, I'd like to speak to you too. Whether it's because you and your husband come from small families, or your kids have no cousins, or your parents are not living or not involved, or the relationships are intentionally limited due to boundaries you have put in place, let me first say how much I admire you. Truly. Todd and I have a nearly ideal scenario as far as the amount of support we have in raising our kids, and it is still *so hard and exhausting*. I simply cannot imagine what it would be like to parent without such support. We have several friends in this position, and we admire these couples so, so much. I can't imagine not being able to ever leave kids with grandparents or drop them at a sister's house to play with cousins. I can't imagine what it would be like to enter into parenting with past baggage, pain, and poor examples, and yet to press forward, parenting in a new, healthy way. What a hard and noble thing, to break unhealthy traditions of the past, forging new roads for your family and your kids. I cannot say that I understand all the nuances and complexities of such a challenge, but I can say that *I see you*. If you are a mom charting a new path alone, you are one of my heroes.

One reader of mine who experienced the heartache of estrangement from her family said it this way: "Growing a life when you're missing your roots feels impossible at times and heartbreaking, but in our weakness, He is glorified. We can be for our kids what *they* need (so as to not create the problem of another generation experiencing that pain and neglect) while giving our own hurt, anger, and instability to Christ for Him to restore, because only He can do that." What beautiful hope this perspective offers in the midst of deep heartache.

The more our culture embraces counter-biblical beliefs and lifestyles, the more essential it is for us as Christian parents to find like-minded families and good mentors. And also people who just love the snot out of our kids. The best hope you have of finding that is in a gospel-centered church. I love hearing stories of people who have found "substitute grandparents." Find friends who value what you value and who don't draw your family apart. It is an incredibly powerful thing for your kids to see other people doing the same (weird) things your family is doing. This is a reinforcement of all you've been teaching them. Your kids benefit from seeing that Mom and Dad aren't the only ones who hold these values; this way of life is real to other people too.

We started this chapter with some fun facts about roots. I've saved the most interesting fact for last. Even though roots often grow very deep, the most important ones for the plant's survival are those *closest to the surface*. I love this parallel to parenting. Even if you don't have deep family roots yourself, I have great news: you can still have the nourishing roots you need to give your kids roots! They will have what you perhaps never did—strong roots where it matters.

SUMMING IT UP

- Family stories, heirlooms, and recipes build a family culture.
- If you have healthy extended family relationships, hold on to them.

TALKING IT OVER

1. What gifts were you given in your "roots," and what are some things you hope not to pass on to your children?
2. Do you have a favorite memory with extended family?

COMING HOME

1. Tell your kids a story about yourself as a child. Whenever I'm stumped, I try to think of something to do with an animal or an injury, and I can usually come up with a story that is remotely interesting. Ha!
2. Ask your kids what recipes they'll long for most when they're grown up and have moved away. For younger kids, just ask what Mommy and Daddy make best!
3. Have a family night and craft that "family mission statement."

One Family's Story: The Renstroms

I don't even remember how I met Natalie. I think it was at a leggings party. I have watched her family bond over the years and love the memories they make! Natalie and her husband, Adam, have three kids.

To us, being a strong family means we're a unit. We do a lot of things together, and when we don't have all five of us, then we're missing a part of our team. Each of our kids brings a different perspective to the table. When you encourage those gifts as parents, the siblings start to respect that in each other as well. It gives them a sense of belonging so that they want to be with us and with each other.

My husband and I come from generationally strong families. Both sets of our parents and grandparents started traditions that continue today. One of my favorite family traditions is our giant extended family vacation. Since the late seventies, my husband's grandparents have funded this weeklong family vacation. It started when their four daughters began to marry. As young newlyweds, they couldn't afford vacations on their own, so the parents would rent a house for them all to stay in as a party of ten. Today it has grown to over fifty-five people! The location and timing have changed over the years, but one thing is certain: the Ward Family Vacation is still happening, and everyone makes it a priority.

A week together with this crowd always has a well-executed plan. Each year, we jot notes of what went well and what didn't, and we save them in a manila folder that the four sisters refer to in weeks leading up to the next vacation. In the folder you also might find everything from the list of theme nights to the number of water bottles purchased to the phone number of the pool cleaning guy. In recent years, "the aunts" (one of them being my mother-in-law) have released some of the reins to the next generation (us). It's been such an undertaking for them all these years, and we want them to enjoy their grandchildren now without having to worry about how this crowd will eat for six days.

One of the aunts still handles the "manila folder," but a daughter-in-law now does the room arrangements and scavenger hunts. Each of the younger families pairs up with another (or two) to buy and cook dinner one night for everyone. I handle the talent show. Another cousin-in-law is a professional photographer and captures beautiful moments all week long. One brother-in-law leads us in worship some mornings, before family devotions led by the uncles. All of us have our talents and bring them to the table.

The key is flexibility. We have found that the fewer plans we have during the day, the better. A couple of beach tents in the sand to sit under and a Bluetooth speaker is all we need to gather us and catch up from the past year. Of course, there is a poster board with a few chores for the cousins, but for the most part it is a well-oiled machine. Most of the upsets during the week are trivial and quickly addressed.

It is not lost on me that this week is *rare*. I am so thankful for a family that is centered on Christ. When I tell others about this week, I can see that they wish their family could do this too. They always feel that they could never get to that point. I remind them that these vacations started as a family of six and that anybody could do it if they made it a priority and put a plan in place!

11

LOYALTY

Growing a Family That's In It for the Long Haul

Home is a safe resting place . . . a refuge,
an asylum of safety and security.

STEVEN BOUMA-PREDIGER AND BRIAN J. WALSH
Beyond Homelessness

Of all the pillar traits of a strong family, loyalty may be the timeliest. Our cultural moment is such that kids need, more than ever, the strength of a family undergirding them. What a time it is to be a kid! When I was in third grade, I was worrying about how to get my teacher to compliment my cursive *p*'s. Cyberbullying was not a thing that was a thing. Can you even imagine being twelve and knowing that at any point, your silly moves and words might be recorded and shared with your entire social group, to be played and replayed and commented on? Imagine living under that type of stress.

Kids younger and younger have an ever-changing, adultlike list of standards to maintain, or they risk being isolated and bullied. My friend said her daughter's teacher outlawed those pricey Stanley water bottles because the third-grade girls were bullying those without them. (*What?*) You could not PAY ME to return to school right now as a kid. No wonder anxiety is through the roof. We cannot pretend this away. It is real.

As parents, it can make us feel powerless and even angry. But we must focus on what we *can* do—provide our children a safe harbor to park in, away from this nonsense. As Kim John Payne so perfectly puts it, "When life gets shaky for your child *out there*, in the world, it's important to make certain life *in here*, within the family sphere, is solid. You may be tempted to direct your attention to what is happening at school [or on the team] or in the neighborhood, but what kids need most is for you to wrap them up in a great big puffy blanket of care and familiarity."[1]

This is what a rich family life does. It is the safe place. At its core, loyalty is a deep, unbreakable bond, a rich gift that holds the family—holds *you*—together. Loyalty says, "I'm with you. You are safe." I can hardly imagine anything in our current moment more deeply beneficial or more comforting. Having a group of people who is for you, for ever and ever, no matter what, is an antidote to the swirling storms we all will face. As a homeschool mom, I take comfort in the fact that my kids have somewhat of a temporary reprieve from the crazy, but I am under no illusions; it is only somewhat, and only temporary. Hurt and sin are inevitable to being a human. It is good to protect our kids from facing some of the cruelty out there but even better to equip them for when they do.

In chapter 4 I told you a little bit about my first engagement. We met when I was in college, and I fell in love. I had never been in love. He was older, and I had harbored a crush on him for two painful years before he told me he liked me too. We had about six months of bliss, during which we became engaged at the top of a skyscraper in New York City. He wasn't exactly who I pictured marrying, but I was so passionately in love that I did not care. Four months after putting the ring on, I started having panic attacks. If I were a counselor, I could give you a more accurate description of what was happening, but my layperson's explanation is this: the subconscious part of me was aware that we would not have a good marriage and was trying to tell this to the conscious part of me. However, the conscious part could not listen. I felt stuck. I could not be happy without him, but it slowly became obvious that I would not be happy with him. There were no choices but despair or panic. I would cry myself to sleep and then start crying again when I woke up. I started skipping classes because I couldn't get my face to look like I wasn't crying. My roommate, my dear, wonderful friend, said, "I'm worried about you. I think you might be depressed." Every night I would shut myself in the broom closet and call my mom. I didn't even have any words. One time she asked, "What if you just say, 'I am not sure I want to marry him.' Can you say that?" I could not say that.

This was my senior year at a college I loved; I was engaged, with "congratulations" posters lining my door. I was a straight-A-except-in-physics student who should have been relishing this season in life. Instead, I was withering away and not functioning. Somehow I ended up on an American Airlines flight home in the middle of the week in the middle of the semester in the middle of my senior year. The only way I did not sob the entire trip was by distracting myself with *Peace like a River*, which a friend had given me. I will forever be grateful to Leif Enger for those five hours of reprieve.

Back at home, my mom took me to the gym and the Cheesecake Factory, and we sat in the sunroom on the navy couches. She walked me through this darkness, not telling me what to do, but waiting for me to say it. By the time I flew back to Pittsburgh, I had clarity. But more significantly, I had perspective. I was not alone, and I was not going to drown. This crisis that had loomed like an atomic bomb, enveloping the entire atmosphere of my life, was rightly sized again. It was a terrible, hard thing, breaking an engagement, but it wasn't everything. It was a storm rumbling in the sky that would maybe get a little darker and louder but then would go away. I had something undergirding me, something stronger and more real than the realest pain I had ever experienced. My family was my perspective.

I want to be this for my kids. When life makes them cower in broom closets because they can't take a deep breath for panic, I want to be the number they can call, even when there are no words. I want them to know there are people who truly have their back. Payne calls this "strengthening family base camp,"[2] and I love that language.

HOW TO BUILD LOYALTY IN THE FAMILY

It truly is a beautiful thing to provide your kids with this kind of supportive environment, but for those of us in the trenches of parenting, "building a strong base camp" might seem impossible, a mirage in the distance, far detached from reality. Take the family car trip, for example. It does not matter how long your drive is; there is something about the last fifty-five minutes of it that is torturous. Everyone brings their worst to the table. There is a minute where the kids are all playing happily with each other, but they are doing this in the MOST ANNOYING way possible so as to make Mom and Dad lose their minds. Then, in the blink of an eye, they turn on one another. These are bleak times of parenting. If you're the kind of parent who writes parenting books, you start really questioning your worth and worthiness. A phrase like "strengthening family base camp" feels like a joke in those moments. Don't despair. This is normal human suffering, and we've all been there. Loyalty is built over the long haul! Here are a few steps that will help you put a strong base camp in place.

Prioritize Having One Another's Backs

If we want to build loyalty among our children, this should be a mantra: "In this family, we stick up for one another. Period." It may seem like I am stating my points strongly in this section; that is just an indication of how important family loyalty is. Make it a family rule that you support your family. Have a zero tolerance policy for kicking someone when they're down. Say someone sits the bench in a game. Our children should know that it is absolutely unacceptable to say to their sibling, "Well, you aren't as good, so it makes sense that you sat on the bench." As the parent, of course, you will find your own way of processing what happened and why, but for the sake of building family loyalty, careless, hurtful passing comments from siblings need to be a NO GO in the home. Nip them in the bud immediately. Pull the critic aside and talk them through their role: "You are a support to your sibling right now. That is all you are."

People always ask me how it is to live on a family compound with ten cousins running around and all my sisters within earshot. I always say it is amazing, because it is amazing. But kids are kids, and of course there are little spats and arguments. There are the "usual suspects": boys versus girls, older versus younger. Regardless, we have stressed over and over that you stick up for your siblings. This is a cardinal rule. You should not join in a laughing session at a sibling's expense. If everyone else wants to pelt your sister with sloppy balls of mud, you had best not join in this nonsense. It is important to note that this conviction does not come naturally to children. There have to be fierce consequences. A sense of loyalty must be cultivated and fought for.

Do Life Together

Making the choice again and again to "come on home," to make these people *our people*, is countercultural in the individualistic times in which we live. It is so easy to be fixated on your own world and hobbies and devices. I really struggle with this, but here's a recent example when God gave me the insight to draw the family together.

In this season of writing a book, life is asking a lot of me. My normal response would be to internalize the stress, letting it seep out in snappy, terse orders to put shoes away and stop arguing while I make dinner. The pressure of running a house, herding everyone to soccer, making kids do their schoolwork, and completing my work projects acts like a vise grip, slowly compressing my anxiety inward until I can take no more.

What does it look like to thrive as a family in this time, to be a loyal bunch, loving and working together? Since we are in the "middle stage" of parenting, with kids who are independent and capable and mostly around, I tried something new. I sat the kids down and talked a little about this writing project. I told them how the extra income would benefit our family. I told them how the book might benefit others and give them ideas of how to grow together in their own families. I reminded them how we already serve Dad as he serves us by working so hard. (At this point I was interrupted with "Just get to the point, Mom. What chores are you giving us?" Gotta love firstborns.) On a dry-erase board, I wrote a quick list of the things I normally do: meals, dishes, cleaning, laundry. I said to the Bossy Firstborn, "You're in charge of this meeting. I'm leaving for a few minutes. Make the list of how you're each going to help. Then tell me at what time your chores will be done and what the consequence will be if the chores aren't done."

And then I walked out. It was a magical meeting. They actually did it. I think it worked because it was more empowering than my normal already-determined chore charts, but also because it created a team culture. They had buy-in. They got the overall meaning. I had invited them into The Work of the Family.

This leads me to the concept of family meetings. Family meetings can get a bad rap. I still remember the urge to roll my eyes when my parents called us to the living room. I have heard that if you serve a special dessert, it ramps up the enjoyment factor. The family meeting in whatever format accomplishes something super significant: it draws the family together. It becomes even more important as kids approach the teenage years, also known as The Years of Self-Centeredness. So this is my advice: don't give up the good old family meeting just because your kids seem to lack enthusiasm.

Instill Loyalty for Life

The most powerful example of loyalty my family will probably ever get was from watching my mom, and my dad, take care of my mom's mother for five years in their home. My Grammy was abruptly moved out of the little trailer in Maryland that she'd lived in for two decades to my parents' home in North Carolina. She was dwindling away. I hadn't seen her for a few years, and my breath caught when I saw her, hunched over and shy of a hundred pounds. But she beamed in recognition when she saw me. My parents hastily converted their office to a little bedroom, shuffling desks and sofas, moving in a bed, and emptying closets. My mom's entire life was similarly rearranged and shuffled. She cared for my Grammy, her mother, like it was the most important calling she could have received.

Grammy had a beautiful, wonderful end of life. Each day, my mom would cheerfully greet her when she woke up, then carefully put in her hearing aids, dress her, brush her teeth, put on her shoes and stockings and a soft cardigan—always a cardigan, "in case there is a chill." Grammy would walk (or rather, be walked) into the kitchen, where her same breakfast was already prepared: a barely warm cup of weak coffee, a plastic cup of juice, toast with a generous serving of butter and jam, a few cheese cubes cut into even smaller cubes, and a handful of berries. This breakfast would eventually be diced into smaller and smaller pieces until the days Grammy stayed in bed and Mom could only coax her to eat mushed-up spoonfuls of mandarin oranges. There were always beautiful things for Grammy to look at: a bird feeder placed just so outside the living room window. A child brought in with a freshly colored picture. A new puzzle on the dining room table.

We weren't living on the family compound during most of those years, so it was Mom and Dad, when he wasn't working, on duty all the time. Most of this happened during Covid, by the way. Imagine being stuck in a house with someone in the throes of dementia. In her lighter moments, Mom would joke that it was like the movie *Groundhog Day*. In the darker moments, we all wondered if Mom would die before Grammy did. Mom got so exhausted and looked such a shadow of her former self that we begged her to get help, to care for herself. Even in the bleakest moments, my mom said the worst part was that she no longer had time and capacity to invest in her grandchildren. Later, when Grammy was gone, there was deep, wrenching sadness in my mom, but there was no guilt. What is more priceless than the satisfaction of completing a job God has given you to do?

It was one of the greatest blessings to see my mother lay down her life, day by day. This season was also a gift for our whole family. I think of so many moments and opportunities for growth that would have been lost had we not had those years with Grammy. All her life, Grammy blessed us. In her final years, she gave us a different kind of blessing: an opportunity to love. There is nothing natural and easy to most of us about speaking with someone seventy or eighty years older than us, answering their repeated questions, deciphering their jumbled speech, feeling their wrinkled hands in ours. Our crew of kids honed this unnatural skill. All of my kids grew up with a tangible reminder that life is not about us.

The grandkids huddled in her room the week before Grammy died, singing "I Am Jesus' Little Lamb." They were in the next room when Grammy passed away. A few of them wanted to see her body. They all sat on the front porch waiting for the people from the funeral home to arrive, to take her body away. Some of them wanted to see the empty room, the empty bed after she was gone. My parents' sweet pastor arrived later and sat on the screened porch with a whole bunch of somber, sniffling cousins who had so many questions: "Where is Great-Grammy now? Can she see us? When will we see her again?" My daughter, who was six at the time, told us later, "I couldn't stop crying when Great-Grammy died, but then the pastor came and talked about heaven, and we stopped crying." It was a gift to our family to walk through the ending of life season, to see this loyalty that lasts right up to the end.

Carry One Another's Burdens

The Bible tells us to carry one another's burdens.[3] We are modeling, as parents, a culture where this is happening. There will be times in the life of a family when someone is struggling. Whether he or she is being left out, gets cut from a team, is struggling in school, faces heartache, breaks a bone, doesn't get invited, has a best friend move away . . . whatever the hardship, as a parent, work to build a support system for your children. Here are a few ways you can do this:

- Name the struggle. As parents, we are often afraid to say something at the dinner table like "So-and-so is struggling right now. She is sad because her friend has been mean to her. This is a really hard thing." Naming it doesn't make it worse; weirdly it makes it better.

- Rally around the struggler. Offer extra love, extra attention. Bring them along on an errand and get them a milkshake. *See* them.
- Envelop them in comforting, soothing routines. As Payne puts it, "The things you do with your child do not have to be elaborate or complicated. . . . When things are going wrong for a child and their lives feel out of shape, 'normal' is exactly what they need."[4] Have a game night. Cook something together. Do a puzzle. Have family dinner—like an extra-good family dinner with a dessert. Author Sally Clarkson often talks about how when one of her children was struggling, a cup of tea, homemade cookies, and an hour or so in Mom's room would gradually bring peace to a troubled soul.

Allow Hardships to Bring You Closer Together

Sometimes multiple people in a family, or the whole family, go through something rough at the same time. These seasons can feel especially dark, and it's even more important to carry each other's burdens. This awfulness can actually be a gift—an opportunity to develop rich bonds.

My favorite college professor walked through cancer while he was teaching us. He would come into class, worn thin and with sunken eyes, dragging the drip chemo behind him as he conjugated Greek verbs on the dry-erase board. Years later I reached out to ask him, "How did you do that? That must have been so hard." I have never forgotten his response: "Many nights I was not sure I would make it to the morning. But those times, while I would never wish them on anyone else, I treasure for myself, because God was so real to me." So often as believers, we experience a hard thing that we would never choose to go through, yet we treasure that time when we look back. Suffering, with the Lord and your family walking with you, is a gift. It can draw you together. It is a time to batten down the hatches, huddle up together, and weather the storm.

As the uncertainty of Covid was at its peak, we moved into a townhome while we built our farmhouse. It was a really hard season. Half of our stuff was in storage. We had said goodbye to all our beloved neighbors. My normally full-of-sunshine daughter became so sullen and limp that I took her to have her blood work done. I was sure she had some underlying chronic infection. Turns out she was just sad.

And then, of course, the pandemic added to the isolation. Somehow that Christmas we unknowingly infected *all four grandparents* with the virus. That was a real high point. A week later my husband got sick, sicker than I've ever seen him. We locked him in our room and taped get-well notes to the outside of his windows. I was very worried about him; we all were. Then we got word that my dear father-in-law had been admitted to the hospital and was rapidly declining. All we could do was cry and pray. In God's kindness, everyone recovered. The following Thanksgiving we wrote on our vinyl tablecloth (where we track the answered prayers from the year), "2020: God protected all of us from Covid." That was an "Ebenezer" of sorts, a marker of God's kindness. That awful time did more to grow us together than twenty adventure hikes. We had no one else but each other.

Cling to Each Other When You Have No One Else

For some families, there is a sense of "aloneness" that's deeper than a temporary quarantine or a season of life without neighbors or a church community. It's an aching loneliness from not having a supportive or close extended family. The parents that I respect most are the ones who have built, brick by brick, these amazing families without those support systems underneath them, or even more remarkably, with crumbling support systems. As I mentioned in chapter 10, if you understand this type of grief, I truly applaud you for what you've achieved.

There is no use denying when things are broken. As parents, we set the tone, and it will be either one of bitterness and despair or of determination and love. During an unsettling time in our country, my mom shared a powerful story. "When I was a little girl, maybe five years old, our barn caught on fire in the middle of the night and burned to the ground. The longest-lasting memory of that night is what my father did for us. After the fire trucks left and neighbors went home, he drew us all together in Mom and Dad's bed and told us we were safe and we could sleep with them. It made everything okay. We were little children and we trusted our daddy to take care of us. It made all the difference. None of us were traumatized by that night or left insecure or anxious, because he sheltered us." I absolutely love this reminder that we parents set the tone for how our children remember hardships.

If you are facing the very difficult challenge of parenting without a good support system, I pray that this only draws you closer together as a family. I pray that you are able to find reprieve when you need it from the demanding work of being a parent. You are building that foundation for your kids to stand on. What beautiful work!

SUMMING IT UP

- Now, more than ever, kids need home to be a safe harbor of people who always have their back.
- Utilize times of hardship, bullying, and loneliness to draw the family closer together.

TALKING IT OVER

1. Has your family ever walked through a time of real hardship and difficulty? How did it strengthen you as a family?
2. What does it mean to you to "strengthen family base camp"?

COMING HOME

1. Tell your kids the stories of the day they were born. Ask the older kids to share with the younger ones what they remember too!
2. Try having a family meeting and putting the kids in charge of some of your tasks. (If you have small children, let one of them lead a meeting about how to help Mommy!)
3. On a white laminated tablecloth, have each family member write answered prayers your family has experienced. Take it out every so often and add to it. (We do this at Thanksgiving!)

One Family's Story: The Brookers

I met Brittany years ago online, and it is amazing to see the Lord work in her family. She is one of my heroes. Brittany is married to Daniel, and they have six children.

In September 2015, my greatest fear became a reality when my husband unexpectedly went to be with the Lord. I became a widow with three boys under three.

I will never forget all the nights of "shutting down" the house by myself, cleaning up after a day full of taking care of my fatherless toddlers and grieving my beloved husband. Then my empty bed reminded me of my empty heart. But I will also never forget the nights when instead of letting self-pity rule my thoughts, I lay on my living room floor and let the tears fall. I told Jesus how lonely I truly was. I told Him how the boys ran to the door when they heard the garage door one evening and cried, "Daddy," even though he had been in heaven for months. I told Him how exhausted I was from making every decision, from being the only parent, and how I missed my person that I wanted to tell everything, to lie in bed with and share stories of the day, excitement for the future, and the hard things of the present. Then I lay down in my pain, and I said, "Jesus I can't even get up without You." I let the ugly tears and the hard questions pour out.

In my utter brokenness, Jesus would meet me. His presence would fill the empty places and remind me I was not walking this road alone. His Word would come to mind and remind me that I would live through this and experience His goodness. He became the treasure in the darkness, the comfort in the pain. My greatest gift in my greatest grief.

In God's kindness, He led me to marry a widower with two children and blend a beautiful family. Our children talk daily about their parents in heaven and enjoy their parents on earth. Today we are "The Brooker Bunch"—two families who have walked through death yet are choosing life. God also gave us the wonderful blessing of a new baby this year. Her life is a testimony to Jesus getting the victory, the final say, bringing joy and beauty instead of just ashes, and all because of His abundant grace. This is a crazy story only God could write. It isn't plan B for our lives; it is God's plan, and He has led us in every hill and every valley.

Blending a family after loss has been something that God has used to humble me and teach me to depend on Him in all things. I've learned that God is the One who can carry the burdens of all these hearts. I can't. God is the One who can knit Daniel and me together. I can't. God is the One who gives me strength to make it through another day. I can't. God heals hearts, bodies, and minds. I can't. No amount of coffee, rest, or breaks is going to get me through a hard season. Jesus is. I need to depend on Christ for it all.

12

FRIENDSHIP

Turning Fighters and Foes into Forever Friends

The advantage of growing up with siblings is
that you become very good at fractions.

ROBERT BRAULT
Short Thoughts for the Long Haul

It's evening. I have a towering stack of dinner dishes on the counter and hot, soapy water bubbling in front of me. It's not my favorite task, but I love my view.

From my kitchen window, I can see Mom and Dad on their front porch. Dad's at the white wicker table, a large glass of ice water in front of him. It's the usual: he's talking, animated; she's listening, thinking. In a few minutes a gaggle of grandkids meanders over from their houses around the cul-de-sac. The littles glide in on scooters, the older ones on skateboards. A pile of metal clinks together in a mishmash in front of Mom and Dad's porch. They'll sit and talk together for a good chunk of time over who knows what. Maybe politics. Maybe the three baby kittens we just adopted, or the naughty goats who keep getting loose. Maybe the kids are updating my parents on their Wiffle ball tournaments in the side yard. The conversation will meander like the barn cats weaving in and out of everyone's legs.

I shake the water off of the spaghetti strainer. To my left, my sister and her husband (dishes washed already, I suppose) are sitting on their own porch, working their way through a bottle of red wine. At the last stop on the cul-de-sac, my other sister waters her tomatoes while her husband reads a book on the front porch. This little mid-July block party will mingle until the sun sets behind our four white farmhouses. I'll have to ring the bell on my front porch to gather in our three kids, layered in dust and sweat, wanting a second dinner, protesting that they don't need showers.

This little neighborhood of ours is a beautiful, magical thing. To have so much family all in one place, willingly, happily—a smack of heaven on this side.

Of course, it's not all magic and peaceful evenings on the front porch. We are human through and through, so we have our share of pity parties, hurt feelings, apologies, tears . . . and that's just the grown-ups. Yet, none of us would trade this experience for all the houses and all the neighbors in the world. What we have here is priceless.

I wonder how my parents brought us to this point. I remember my mom saying when we were in the thick of the teenage years, "One day, your siblings will be your best friends." And I would think, *THESE PEOPLE? THERE IS NO WAY.* I was a terrible sister, actually. I had a streak of smacking my siblings that honestly lasted well into middle school. My sisters and I would have some epic blowups over the usual complaints: favorite sweaters borrowed without approval, bathrooms locked so no one else could get in to do their makeup, the coveted shotgun seat stolen from someone else who had claimed it . . . I loved my siblings beyond words and was a giant brat for a good 75 percent of my childhood.

So I wonder again, how did it happen? How was it possible to transform normal, sinful humans into a family of people who have one another's backs and actually—miracle of miracles—don't just love each other but like each other, willingly spending time together? How does such a miracle transpire?

This, of course, is where the rubber really meets the road in parenting. Nothing can disarm your happy confidence in facing a Saturday like screaming and crying from the playroom. Few things are quite so unsettling as a child who is flat-out malicious toward his siblings. And nothing stumps a mom like that age-old question, how do you get your kids to get along? (And not just "get along" so they can keep playing the Wii, but to really and truly be genuine friends?)

I assure you, this is possible. You and your husband can confidently create a family culture that will be life-giving for years and years. All it takes is some long-term dreaming, a good plan, and plenty of tools for troubleshooting when your plan seems to be blowing to smithereens.

BENEFITS OF HAPPY FAMILIES

Most parents are drawn to the idea of their kids getting along because—let's face it—it makes our lives one thousand times easier. It is inconvenient to have arguing kids. It stinks to have to referee squabbles, administer punishments, and listen to convoluted, whining stories about who did what and why and whose fault it was to begin with. This is all beyond annoying, and the idea of children playing nicely upstairs so you can drink your coffee in peace is quite appealing.

However, this peace and quiet is merely a side benefit of good sibling relationships, and not in fact the primary gift to everyone. Healthy, deep family bonds accomplish so much for the individual members of the family that you just can't achieve otherwise. There is no substitute.

Kids who grow up with strong relationships in their family of origin function in life with a massive advantage. They have friends—built-in and always. They have an environment and habits of (mostly) healthy conflict resolution, and they experience lower rates of depression later in life.[1] They have holiday and weekend plans—fun ones, ones you can bring guests into proudly. They have more confidence and experience less loneliness during the tumultuous years of arriving into adulthood. Strong sibling relationships stave off loneliness and anxiety throughout adulthood, even into our older adult years.[2] What a gift we give our families when we gift them people who are absolutely, without a doubt, for them, no matter what happens.

HOW TO GROW FRIENDSHIPS WITHIN YOUR FAMILY

If it feels like it would take a miracle for your kids to ever be best friends, do not despair. If you look (or listen) to your crew and think you've failed massively at family bonding, fear not! It is not too late. In all those years I was growing up, my parents were patiently sowing the seeds for deep family roots. These roots were growing deep, despite the storms aboveground!

So, how do we grow this type of family culture? It may feel a monumental job. I remember when my angelic firstborn discovered that the little baby who had been visiting our home

- was going to stay,
- was equally part of the family,
- could move around, and
- was very interested in the toys that had previously belonged solely to himself.

This previously angelic firstborn was not so for long. It's annoying to have a sibling. Of course, one day something happens, usually around year two or three of Baby Number Two's life. There is a moment—and it's amazing—when your two children discover that they may actually enjoy playing together. The first occurrence lasts about seventeen seconds, and you have likely wasted nine of those seconds grabbing your phone to record it, but nevertheless IT HAPPENED. The next decade or so is a whirling dance of

- liking each other,
- not liking each other,
- with emphasis likely on the latter.

This is normal. As you prepare to build those solid, life-giving relationships within the family, a few steps and reminders will prove helpful. And PS: I have a friend whose kids just seem to be magically best friends, without effort. This is not the way things go in our house. Maybe that makes you feel a little better? This isn't a diet-advice-from-someone-who-has-never-had-to-lose-a-pound kind of thing. This is advice from someone who has had to work at it. I feel your pain.

Frequently Remind Everyone That God Chose Your Family

Do you ever look around the dinner table and wonder how in the world *this* group of people ended up together in a family? I think it's super helpful to remind ourselves (and our kids) that it is no accident. Just as God chose you specially to be your kids' mom, He chose each member of the family, with purpose and kindness. Which means—He has a reason! Sometimes it feels like there is no reason or that the reason is to frustrate you endlessly. Sometimes it feels like we are all so different and so alike in all the wrong ways. I find deep comfort in recognizing God's hand in orchestrating our family. This has several implications.

First, each of us is naturally a gift to the others, and this is an act of God's kindness to us. Take a minute to have your kids appreciate how everyone in the room is a blessing to them. I love my middle child's ability to put together IKEA furniture, because I can't build something to save my life. And what a cheery soul my daughter is to me on my anxious days. Encourage your kids to appreciate how God chose to bless your family with each member, and thank Him for His gift.

The second and less happy fact is that there are things that will frustrate us about one another, but this is God's way of making us holy. The idea that life isn't about happiness but holiness is going to be extremely hard to explain to, say, a four-year-old. I would explain it like this: "I know you're upset that your baby sister messed up your LEGOs. That is frustrating! Let's pray and ask God for help. Dear God, thank You for Sissy. Please help me love her. Amen."

Boom. Sanctification for a four-year-old. And I'll be honest—I have prayed some very similar prayers for the frustrating people in my life as recently as yesterday!

Cast the Vision (Plan Your Future Family Vacation)

It's important that every member of your family be very clear what the goal is: we are going to be best friends in twenty years. After all those times of my mom saying it, we eventually believed it. When I read Nicholeen Peck's *Parenting: A House United*, we had a family meeting at which we sat down and thought forward twenty years, to our vacation.[3] Where would we be? Who would be there? What would we be doing? When you picture the person in the next room as your adult best friend, it does lend some context to how you handle it when they crumple your special drawing. This is our story—we are best friends, and we *will* be best friends. We have a vacation to go on.

I have also found it helpful to compare and contrast families we know. Sometimes I'll list actual names and sometimes I leave it more imaginary. I may say, "Do you love playing with your cousins?" (Long pause as they reflect that, yes, they do.) "Well, if Aunt Julie and I fought all the time and had a terrible relationship, how much would you see your cousins?" (Another long thoughtful pause and a gulp.) Or I may say, "I have a friend who does not talk to his brother at all. They live in the same town, and they don't even get together at Christmastime. It's really sad!"

This also helps with long-term vision casting. Because of course, the relationships you build now are the same ones that you have later. Between you and me, there is a lot of time to iron out these kinks, but our kids need to understand the beauty of what they've been given. A sibling! A best friend in the making! A future vacation partner! This is the life we are building. These people are precious.

Expect and Accept Difficulty

As a mom, sometimes I find myself being surprised when there is sin in our home. Why should this surprise me? Sometimes I find myself being shocked when I realize anew that I am the one in charge of untangling the mess. Again, why should this unnerve me? I wanted to have children. I wanted to raise them. Raising sinful human beings is a job that *feels* like a job. It is not something you can do in between unloading the silverware and grinding the coffee. It takes time and energy. Do I allot this energy in my life? Or do I feel annoyed when parenting—the real stuff of parenting, like discipline and conversation—takes up my time? A sign in my sister's kitchen says, "Children are not a distraction from the important work. They are the most important work."

A crucial step of achieving really awesome and life-giving family relationships is to not be annoyed when it takes effort and time. Accept it. Go ahead and plan to delegate some of your brainpower toward this task. When a wonderful opportunity to build sibling relationships comes up, do not be surprised. It will rarely come when you are motivated and interested in parenting, like right at this moment when you are reading this book. More often it will come when you are, say, enjoying an adult conversation or knee-deep in a really intense job, like scrubbing iron buildup out of your toilet. Children have antennae for these moments. When your children are being mean, or someone is crying, or a fight needs Adult Engagement, see the situation for what it is: the most important task you will take on all day (which is to say, building a strong family).

Pay Attention

Once you've decided that building a strong family culture is worth it, and once you have decided to allot some time and energy toward this work, something else will happen. You will start paying attention, and you will start noticing things. They may be surprising things. You might notice that things are not what they seem. Maybe, for one example, the "innocent and well-behaved" one was sliding mean glances toward his sister. Maybe you have a doted-on, well-behaved child who actually delights in seeing others get in trouble. Maybe, to put it another way, it is almost like all of your children are equally sinful and equally human. That would be a novel thought.

There are interesting dynamics in any family. There is always the kid who gets in trouble more often. There is always the Perpetual Annoyer and the Perpetual Annoyed. I have found it worth my time to consider why the misbehavers are who they are. What is it like to be them? How does everyone treat them? Do they start out the day with everyone expecting them to be unpleasant? What would it look like to rewrite the story for them? What would it look like to wake up and give each child a fresh slate? Perhaps you have tried this, and twelve minutes after breakfast The One Who Is Usually Naughty reminds everyone of his reputation. It takes time to undo these patterns.

Notice what is happening in your family. Observe. Walk a mile in everyone's shoes. Don't be biased. Look for ways that each child is perpetuating unhealthy relationships. And look for reasons that people are acting the way that they are acting. It could be a million different scenarios. Maybe it's a teenager who is lonely, and it comes out as grumpiness. Maybe a middle child feels overlooked and acts out in anger. Maybe someone is relishing being the "good child" and needs a reminder not to delight in evil but rejoice in the good. Or maybe someone (everyone?) is just being naughty and needs Jesus and lots of prayers.

Of course these are all oversimplifications without clear-cut solutions, but your main job at this point is to start noticing and to see things you may not have been seeing.

Give Everyone a Job

Everyone needs a job, and I don't just mean chores. I mean a personalized, individualized, "just-for-you" life mission to help build the family culture. Each child should feel challenged and have ownership for their unique role. There was a certain time when our oldest was informed that it was the most important role of his life to be a good big brother to his younger brother. We fleshed this out—what did this look like? It looked like encouraging him. It looked like not beating him at every game, because how would that feel, to lose every game just because someone was always bigger and quicker? It looked like building his brother up. We sat our firstborn down and said, "This is your job. God made you a big brother, and here's how you do it poorly, and here's how you do it well."

Everyone in the family has an empowering role to play. Focus on their gifts and possibilities. Can they be a helper to Mommy? If one of the younger kids looks up to them, can they invest in that relationship? Make it very clear what everyone should be working on. This should be a "do" not a "don't." Come up with an exciting twist on it. This can apply to children from two to seventeen. If you can't think of a good job for someone, pray about it.

Show Zero Tolerance for Rudeness

When prioritizing healthy sibling relationships, make sure you are prepared to put your "money" where your mouth is. This means actually inconveniencing your kids, and thereby unfortunately yourself, when a relationship needs fixing. People who are perpetually mean to their siblings should not be allowed to happily glide through life with a full social calendar. There are two sayings that I repeat most often in our home: "Please shut the door" (because am I even a mom if I don't say this seven times before lunch?) and "If you can't play nicely with your siblings, you can't play with anyone else."

My mom always says, "Loving the people in your family is the hardest job in the world." And the most important! It takes some wisdom and nuance to resolve the root of the problem. Sometimes a child needs time alone. Sometimes she has something festering that she needs to vocalize. Sometimes she needs to do the hard, annoying work of investing in her sibling.

My kids aren't surprised if I tell them they can't do some Fun Thing but instead need to spend time with their siblings. They are, however, annoyed. Realizing that God made you the mom empowers you to ignore their frustration and do the right thing—in this case, prioritizing healthy family dynamics over a fun social calendar.

Name and Fight Self-Centeredness

Family bonding, like most true friendship, involves a give-and-take, a willingness to die to self at times. It involves giving of your time and your love when you may not feel like it. So, do not be shocked when someone (typically an older kid) isn't pumped about little sibling time. Address it head-on: "Yes, I know you don't want to play Catan right now. I don't either! But this means a lot to your siblings. I love seeing you make hard choices like your dad. You are growing up to be such a wonderful young man."

One motivation for me to have these hard conversations was the realization that I don't want to raise kids who are so self-centered with their own lives that they don't ever come on home. This starts now. Attaching to one another is a choice we make. We can train our kids in this skill, but we have to start by seeing resistance for what it is: selfishness.

Make the Space

A few years ago, a child in our house got a consequence of twenty-four hours with no outside friend time. Around hour seven, the most incredible thing happened. Straining my ears, I heard this child upstairs happily playing pet store with younger siblings and cousins. This child had nothing better to do so probably thought, *What the heck. I'll bring my stuffed lizard into the pretend pet clinic. Why not?* After seven hours all by one's lonesome, pet store, a game that hitherto would have been ignored or even mocked, apparently sounded downright interesting.

This reminded me of the power of good, old-fashioned boredom. After all, this is a concept I praised at length in my last book, *Let Them Be Kids*.[4] Our culture is dead set on having us schlep kids back and forth nonstop, and when we're not schlepping, we're all being mentally stimulated by some sort of screen or noise. Mental white space, among the many, many gifts it provides, creates room for deep friendships to grow. So to put it directly: if your kids are not bonding well, or worse, are at each other's throats, evaluate your schedule. Put a hold on the nonessentials for a bit. Let your kids be bored. *Pro tip: This may not be well received. Expect the question "Wait—what? Why are we stuck in the house? Why can't I go anywhere? What's the reason, Mom and Dad?" Stand strong. Use the old "Because I said so" if you have to. You're doing the right thing. They need a break.

Mind the Gaps

If sibling friendships are naturally difficult to foster, it can feel even *more* tricky when the age span is wide or kids seem not to share similar interests. I love seeing families handle this well. My friends Lindsey and Shawn have four kids, ages four to seventeen. When Lindsey was thirty-nine, she found out she was pregnant with their fourth child, in a complete surprise. As a result, their life is an amusing dance that includes things like dropping one kid off at preschool on the way to get another child her driver's license. On the kids' homeschool days, Lindsey requires her big kids to have thirty minutes of "big brother or big sister camp" in their day, during which time they are 100 percent focused on their little sibling, doing whatever they want—pretending, playing blocks, and so on.

"There's really no magic bullet," Lindsey says. "We just do the things and bring all the people. We're going to stick together as a family." She acknowledges it's hard—it's not natural for the big kids to want to hop in on little kid fun. She often reminds her oldest kids that they got a chance to do all the "little kid things" and that this is their chance to let their sister experience the magic of that too!

As your kids get older, they may not naturally play together, especially when they start getting their own interests, activities, or friends. You may need to be proactive as a parent about carving out sibling time. Like my friend Lindsey, I will often include "play with sibling for thirty minutes" on a child's chart of things they must do before heading out to play. I brainstorm with them

Activities That All Ages Can Enjoy

Thanks to my friends with kids of all ages for helping me out with this list! Of course, none of these awesome ideas eliminates the need for good, old-fashioned Being a Good Sport. Praise those older kids when you see them doing it; it doesn't come naturally!

- a rodeo
- sporting events
- board games
- puzzles
- bonfires
- camping
- bike rides
- hiking
- sundae bars
- movies
- reading aloud / audiobooks
- family shows like *Minute to Win It*, *Wheel of Fortune*, *Are You Smarter Than a Fifth Grader?*

things that count as playing. One time the brainstorming involved locking two grumpy children out of the house until they could come in with a list of five hobbies they shared. I do not necessarily recommend this, but it was a thing that happened.

I've also heard people say that when their kids get older, they will fund any adventures between siblings. In other words, if you want to go to dinner as a group of siblings, I'll buy the pizza; if you want to bowl, it's on me. I tried a version of this for two younger kids whose friendship I am really working to build. One Saturday, I had some free time and just these two kids at home. I told them, "Kids, if you play Monopoly all morning and it does not end in a giant mess of a fight, I will take you out to Chick-fil-A for lunch! If the winner is a good winner and not obnoxious, the winner earns an ice-cream cone for dessert. If the loser is a good loser and doesn't whine, the loser earns their ice-cream cone." This worked! They played a wonderful game of Monopoly, and both had great incentive to work on these character traits.

If the word "bribe" came to your mind when you read my plan, I'd like to speak to that. Bribes are different from external motivation. We all work for external motivation and incentives. We are wired to experience external motivation. I think it's okay to use these types of incentives as long as you are also working (in different scenarios) to ensure that your kids can accept a "no" answer nicely.

Plan Family Game Nights

I couldn't end this chapter without a mention of games! There's nothing like a good game to bring a whole family together. Or tear one to pieces. (My husband and I have yet to play a game of Scattergories that hasn't ended in a fight. He is that annoying player who writes things like "purple polka partying panda" for "found in an attic" and expects to get four points. I have nothing to say to this.) We are truly fortunate to live in a time with an abundance of creative, inexpensive, and fun games that all ages can play. Often, we might assume that since games are fun and recreational, our kids should naturally want to play them. Maybe we get frustrated if there is pushback, or maybe we don't attempt to make it happen if they don't want to play. I have no problem with motivating, encouraging, and making my kids play games sometimes. Often they don't initially want to play but then have so much fun doing it.

If you have very little ones, game night is not going to be this calm, mentally stimulating, quiet evening with a bowl of popcorn slowly savored. It might be chaos. Lean into the chaos and don't work against it! Try very active games, such as Simon Says, Red

Awesome Family Games

- Apples to Apples
- Balderdash
- Carcossonne (like Catan but shorter)
- Charades
- Chicken Dominoes
- Codenames
- Dixit (like Apples to Apples with pictures)
- Dominion
- Five Crowns
- 5-Second Rule
- Forbidden Island
- Minute to Win It games
- Monopoly Deal
- Pictionary
- Scattergories
- Catan
- 7 Wonders games
- Shut the Box
- Telestrations
- Ticket to Ride
- Trekking the National Parks (similar to Ticket to Ride)
- What Do You Meme? Family Edition (but still go through the cards and take some out)
- Who's Most Likely To . . .

Light Green Light, Twister, The Floor Is Lava (actually a game you can buy!), Crocodile Dentist Game, Perfection, Sturdy Birdy, and Headbands. In our adult minds, we think game night is this long thing. But for little ones, it could be a legitimately great night if you do a few quick games and eat dessert. With this small start, you're forming a habit you can grow later.

If you have little kids and big kids, don't feel bad putting the littles to bed (or in a Pack 'n Play) while the older kids play games with you. In other words, it's great to include the whole family, but if the littles are ruining the atmosphere to the extent that you can't play a game, they don't always need to be included. One family I knew always wrote the date and the winner of each game on the inside of the game box. What a memento you'd have inside your Catan box after years and years!

SUMMING IT UP

- If kids can't be nice to their siblings, there should be consequences.
- Sometimes there are hidden power dynamics at work between siblings—be observant and look for what's really happening behind the scenes.

TALKING IT OVER

This time, the discussion questions are for the whole family!

1. What is your favorite thing to do with each member of your family?
2. How old will everyone be in twenty years? What do you think you'll each be doing then? Where would you want to go on vacation together?
3. Why do you think God made you a big sister/brother to ___________? (Get them each thinking about how they are uniquely wired to help, encourage, take care of, cheer up, teach, play with each of their siblings.)

COMING HOME

1. Think of someone you trust who loves your family. For whatever family dynamic is frustrating to you right now, ask this person their take on the situation.
2. Spontaneously have an "only play with your siblings day" after your kids have had a season with too many social activities. They each have to play with a sibling for thirty minutes. Give them ideas such as have a treasure hunt, play Candyland, play dolls, or read a book together.
3. For younger kids, utilize a kindness reward jar. Every time they do something kind for a sibling, they get a token in the jar. They should be able to fill the jar and earn a reward about once a week. The prize: a date with Mom or Dad.

One Family's Story: The Turners

My friend Amy discovered she was surprise-pregnant when her oldest was fourteen. She and her husband now have four kids, ages two to sixteen. She has such great insight for making family time work for all ages.

Growing up neither of us came from families that emphasized healthy family and sibling relationships. We decided early on that this was going to be a goal in raising our family. I often see parents struggling with family time. First, they have high expectations that no one will fight or complain and it will be all unicorns and sparkles. The reality is that our kids are human, so hold loosely to expectations. Our kids have all different temperaments: leaders and sensitive kids, slow kids and fast kids, little and big. Just roll with it and keep the goal in mind. This isn't a time to focus on correction. Laugh away little arguments. The kids will usually pick up on that and move on as well.

Parents also struggle because they only focus on togetherness on family nights, and the rest of the time everyone ignores each other and goes off in separate directions. Togetherness needs to be a constant focus—school, projects, dinner, chores, yard work, reading, errands, or siblings' sports events. When you do life together, you come to like the same things, and it becomes natural to then have a "fun night" together. If you don't encourage togetherness from an early age, kids will eventually resist it.

We also need to let God purge us of selfishness. It's easier to make dinner alone, shop alone, send everyone to separate schools, buy the frozen pizza, have twelve TVs so everyone watches their own show, but that's not why we had families. This season is almost always going to require sacrifice. How kind of God to model that for us. Togetherness is a habit, not an event. It does get harder as they get older. It's often more "event" focused, but the habit has been laid and that was what we wanted. Eventually they will have their own families and hopefully create a legacy and keep coming home for more.

Here are some of our favorite things to do as a whole family!

Game night. Fun ones that get us all laughing and on the same "playing field" like Heads Up! or Taco Cat Goat Cheese Pizza. Littles are teammates with a parent.

Flashlight hide-and-seek, indoors or outdoors. Littles can team with a parent.

LEGO competition. Decide on a category like space or farm or epic bathrooms. Everyone builds for a set time. Pick a winner, but also give awards for "most creative" or "used the most pieces."

Work on a project together. Build a tree house, zip line, firepit—something your family would then enjoy together.

Supermarket sweep. Break into pairs or teams, with a parent on each team or older kids against parents. Each team gets a specific grocery list and a cart, and it's a race to get every item and come back to the checkout first. No running or yelling, of course!

13

GRACE

Help and Hope for the Hard Days

One's own home is the place where love must first be practiced before it can truly be practiced anywhere else.

MIKE MASON, *The Mystery of Marriage*

I will never be half the woman that my mom is. If I could inherit three characteristics of hers, this is what I would choose. One, her decorating. She will spend years (truly, years) settling on the perfect fabric for a chair. She will get a vision for a room, and when she's finished, everything will seamlessly flow together, creating this perfect, inviting space that's both gorgeous and welcoming. Two, her hospitality. Even though she is an introvert, her parties are the most epic, well-executed gatherings. The food is always carefully chosen, beautifully displayed, and somehow the perfect temperature. It makes you feel rather special and loved. My sisters and brother have picked up some of these skills. And then there's me . . . usually asked to bring a bag of ice to the party.

The third and most important trait of my mother's that I want to emulate is grace. I have been taking mental notes over the past few decades as I have watched both of my parents, and in particular my mother, embody how to love and forgive and give. There have been plenty of times I thought (watching from the sidelines) that there was *too much* giving, too much patience. But after thirty years, the proof is in the pudding. When people (random people, like the florist delivery lady) realize that my parents are living on thirty acres with their daughters and grandkids, they always say something like "Wow. How did you get so lucky?" There is an element of luck, I suppose (Mom would say it's God's undeserved blessings), but my parents are reaping what they have sown. I can see what is reaped from this kind of loving, this kind of life. I want that fruit for my own family.

My dad had his own special contributions to our family life. Nobody is a bigger cheerleader for his kids and grandkids than he is. He has literally been thrown off of soccer fields, not for angry yelling, but for overly excited cheering. Random fans will glare him down, ask him to be quiet, and he will say, "I am here to cheer for my grandkids." Truly, I don't remember him ever saying a critical word when I was young. I take that back; I do remember some critical words, but they mainly centered around candy wrappers left in the minivan. He really, really hated candy wrappers in the minivan. Unfortunately, our minivan was destined to be disgusting.

Dirty cars notwithstanding, Dad was abounding in grace during our growing-up years. He loved to believe the best about us. In his eyes, we could accomplish anything. I don't know that this is an attitude that can be replicated; maybe you either have it or you don't. This morning, I asked my mom how my dad could have such boundless energy when he subsisted on cheese Danish and Jersey Mike's turkey sandwiches. "Genetics," she said dryly. Similarly, we may not all have a natural bent for being epic cheerleaders for our children. I am just telling you what his approach did for us. It made us want to become what he thought we were.

I've mentioned that he was gone a lot when we were growing up. We missed him terribly. But one thing that helped was that when he was home, he was HOME. He was always larger-than-life, filling the room with spirited banter and stories. No one can tell a story like my dad can. He can tell you a story in which the plotline is essentially that someone bought a Coke at the gas station, and you will be hanging on every word for ten minutes of this breathtaking tale.

Whereas Dad is larger-than-life, Mom is a quiet, steady presence. Our family thrived because when Dad was gone, she single-handedly kept the ship afloat. Raising us was all she did. Some people would say she should have had more hobbies, more friends. Maybe. It seems like it has worked out fine for her in the end.

As I write to you, I feel the need to emphasize that I am not a pastor or a counselor. I'm just a mom who had a really good mom (and dad) to learn from. As is my style, I do want to share some facts and thoughts from the experts about the importance of grace for our families, but I also want to share with you what I have observed and learned from both my parents.

When I look back over my life, a handful of lessons from Mom about grace stand out. My guess is that they might be less relevant to you if you're in that stage of bribing someone with fruit snacks to pee in the potty. But I hope you'll stick these thoughts in your "back pocket" for the middle school stages and beyond. Maybe these themes will also be helpful as you and your husband navigate your extended family relationships.

FAMILY: HARDEST AND MOST IMPORTANT TO LOVE

Mom is constantly reminding us that our mission in life is to love our family. It is easy (I know from experience) to be someone who is nice to people Out There and a big jerk to the people you see every day. Mom has a zero tolerance policy for this. She often says, "The hardest people to love are the people in your family." She says that, not only because we are a loud and selfish bunch in particular, but because that is just true of life. The people you see all the time, who change the channel while you are watching, borrow your sweatshirt without asking, chew with their mouths open, take too long in the shower, eat the last piece of bacon, grate on your nerves with the same old habits—these are the ones it is hardest to love. But Mom would say, *"These are the ones God has given us to love."* What she was doing was teaching us to hate hypocrisy—the fake sort of love that only loves in public, in snippets.

My father-in-law, when he sees me correcting a behavior in one of my kids, always says with a smile, "It only takes two thousand repetitions to make a new habit!" This is likely the number of times we were given my mom's "love your family" talk, so maybe my father-in-law is about right. Mom was constantly reminding us when we were annoyed or angry with one another that this was the very time we were to live out our faith. I want to follow her example and continue impressing upon our kids how important it is to show love to one another. When we tell them to be kind, it's not some idea we parents came up with to make our lives easier. (Although, it does . . . and we could have.) No—this authentic kindness thing is *God's* idea, God's rule.

I can see how this is especially applicable to people-pleasing types, since I am one of those. If you have a child who loves Jesus and is doing all the "right things"—helping out with VBS or reading her Bible or earning some Christian character award—but struggling to love her siblings, it might be good to break out this reminder. It is hardest to love the people in your own house, but it's a sad hypocrisy that thinks it doesn't matter.

GUARD YOUR SPEECH

People used to say to me that the baby and toddler years were the easy ones, and I thought that was nonsense. What in the world could be harder than simultaneously nursing a baby and diapering a squirmy toddler when you're sleep-deprived? But I have to say—I get it now. As our kids grow, the issues become more serious, the stakes higher. The conflict is more real, with the potential to be more dangerous and harmful. The conversations start getting more complex, fast. This is where the virtue of grace and discretion in speech can be extremely important in preserving strong family bonds. I'm sure I don't need to tell you that you can't unsay things. Of all the differences between Mom and me, probably the biggest is that when I have something to say, I say it. Mom is very measured with her words. She has said to me probably a hundred times, "You will never regret something you didn't say." When I think about the amount of restraint she has shown over the years when she was worried, concerned, hurt, angry, confused . . . it seems a superhuman power. She would agree and would tell me that God has given her grace to do this.

When I look at Scripture, guarding our speech seems like a profoundly biblical notion. Look at these gems I pulled out of Proverbs:

"In the multitude of words sin is not lacking, but he who restrains his lips is wise."

"He who guards his mouth preserves his life, but he who opens wide his lips shall have destruction."

"Whoever guards his mouth and tongue keeps his soul from troubles."[1]

I think the health of my family of origin can be attributed in large part to my parents' profound discretion over when to speak and to their wisdom in choosing to defuse tempers instead of adding fuel to a fire. I have watched them take time for prayer and thoughtfulness instead of rushing to address a problem that I thought needed to be dealt with immediately. Whenever I feel overwhelmed by an issue with someone I love, unsure of what to do, I think of Mom's constant refrain: "Pray, pray, pray." When we face a parenting conundrum with our own kids, I wonder what would happen if we prayed before speaking, before acting. I wonder what kind of fruit would grow if we, like my mom, encouraged our kids to guard their speech with one another.

Of course, there are times when you need to speak. I don't want to convey that my family stuffed things under the rug. In fact, I am quite proud to tell you that one of my spiritual gifts is having hard conversations. What's that you say? That's not a spiritual gift? Oh well, I do think I excel at it nevertheless. Our extended family doesn't avoid conflict or spirited discussions, and I think that this may feel stressful for the handful of peacemakers in our bunch, especially during election years or weeks when PMS is happening simultaneously. Mostly, we are able to discuss all manner of things and still be close friends.

In researcher Herbert Lingren's famous study on strong families, he noted that in healthy families,

> Family members could talk and listen to each other in a non-critical, non-judgmental, and non-threatening manner. They used positive, supportive communication skills. They listened with their hearts as well as their ears. They shared and respected each other's ideas without putting them down. They were able to say what they felt without insulting or criticizing the other person. They talked about what made them feel angry or sad or pleased. Strong families did have conflicts and members did argue. But they took the time to talk out their differences and share their feelings so as to better understand each other.[2]

A Lifeway article concluded similarly: "A healthy family enjoys open, frequent communication. No question is inappropriate, no opinion is disrespected, and no subject is considered off limits. Important, life-determining subjects are naturally intermingled with the mundane."[3]

These descriptions remind me of a big family dinner at my parents' house. The discussion might jump from the ideal crispiness of bacon to electric vehicles to whether kids should go to college. My husband (one of the minority peacemakers) would probably say that some of us (*ahem*) could work on being more respectful of differing opinions. Touché. I have had to do my share of apologizing and forgiving.

The Bible speaks about not letting a "root of bitterness" grow,[4] and that phrase has always stuck in my head as an ideal I try to hold. Here's a small example. For the past few weeks, I've noticed that one of my sisters seemed grumpy toward me. I finally said (and probably not in the most gracious way), "Are you mad at me about something?" She was able to tell me that it felt like I was always in a hurry, always leaving, always stressed. That hurt. But I am glad she told me, and our relationship is better for having "gotten it out there."

Our family definitely has had some difficult conversations and even a few epic behind-the-scenes blowups. I do not think you can have true community without occasional blowups and conflict . . . At least, I have not experienced it that way. This makes grace even more vital.

FORGIVE, FORGIVE, FORGIVE

As my mom says, when conflict arises, "You forgive and forgive and forgive." If she has said it once, she has said it a thousand times. And it makes sense. You can have all the movie nights you want, visit all the national parks, but if your family is unable to forgive, there is not much hope for a real, lasting bond. Still, it is hard to be the one forgiving or the one who needs the forgiving. I sin a lot. Everyone sins a lot. You absolutely cannot be shocked by the need to forgive your family members over and over again . . . or to ask for forgiveness. It is a muscle that needs strengthening over and over again.

I have watched my mom model this profoundly. There have been more than a few times that it seemed she had the right to be truly angry with others. We were angry *for* her. She would say with emotion, "Girls, I don't want to hold on to this bitterness. I don't want this. Jesus has forgiven me so much. I have to forgive." I have watched with my own eyes as God replaced her well-justified anger with love and grace. Whenever I am tempted to hold a grudge, I think of her example.

RELATIONSHIP ABOVE ALL

As I watched my parents discipline, discuss, confront, ignore, and forgive, I have seen one thread weaving through it all: preserving the relationship. When I'm hot and bothered about something, Mom is so fond of asking, "What is your end goal here?" I will take a deep breath and begrudgingly admit that snapping someone's head off will not further my purpose. That end goal? I want a strong, godly family with healthy relationships. My mom has this incredible gift for constantly seeing past the immediate issue to the overarching goal we are trying to accomplish. It is a very relational approach, and it holds true.

We cannot bark someone into the Kingdom. We won't badger, berate, or guilt them off the wrong path and onto the right one. But we don't give up on people either. We stay connected with them, extending patience, giving room for the Holy Spirit to work. When we address problems, we do so with a firm undergirding of "We are in this for the long haul, you and me." It is a foundational shift that changes everything about everything.

When we think about dealing with our kids and about their difficult ups and downs in life, preserving the relationship is essential. Gordon Neufeld and Gabor Maté speak to this in *Hold On to Your Kids*, explaining the value of relationship for kids going through a rebellious streak. "It is when things are the roughest that we should be holding on to our children the most firmly. . . . If we parents allow ourselves to become alienated, we will burn the only bridge by which the child can return. It takes a saint to not be alienated, but . . . sainthood may be what we are called to."[5]

GOD GIVES THE STRENGTH

All of this makes sense on a cognitive level, but it is so STINKIN' hard to follow through. It is hard for us and hard for our kids. If you're like me, you may one day arrive at the depressing realization that despite all your preaching about love and kindness and friendship, your kids just don't seem to get it. They often don't want to love. They resist forgiving. They'd rather just be bitter and grumpy. There is no grace. Just because we know we *need* to love doesn't mean we can *do* it . . . not on our own anyway.

Maybe you find yourself in a conversation with a child, and after all your scolding, they are just as dead set as before on telling you how awful, awful, awful and annoying, annoying, annoying the other kids are. I know what it's like to look someone in the face and see not an ounce of grace or kindness. That's a scary feeling for a parent. But it shouldn't surprise us. I find deep comfort in the fact that when God gives us the command to love, He gives us the ability to keep the command as well. To quote my hero, Corrie ten Boom, "I discovered that it is not on our forgiveness any more than on our goodness that the world's healing hinges, but on His. When He tells us to love our enemies, He gives, along with the command, the love itself."[6]

We should normalize praying with our kids for the strength to do what we are asking them to do. They need His grace, as we do.

COMING HOME

I began this book by telling you about my Grammy. As she lay in my parents' home in her final hours, my dad tenderly recited to her a passage from John 14: "In My Father's house are many mansions. . . . I go to prepare a place for you."[7]

Minutes later, Grammy went Home.

She spent her life planting seeds, growing a family. Some of her work was fruitful and reaped blessings. Some of it was not.

As I write this, I am one week from turning forty-three. I am not old and wrinkled in my bed. I am not really thinking about heaven. I am thinking about what I am making for dinner tonight and the things we have to pack for a soccer game. I know that you, too, are in the thick of it, building your home, building a family.

It is not fun to think that you and I are approaching the place Grammy was. In truly a blink, our short lives will be over. We could ignore this fact and try not to think about it (which is what I mostly do).

But we could also number our days and gain a heart of wisdom.[8] How does thinking about Going Home—having an eternal perspective—impact growing our family?

First, it makes the small things seem small again. In light of eternity, spats with our husband or grumpiness with a child hit us in a different way. When the vacation gets canceled, when the family night ends in a tantrum, when a child is in a funk . . . remembering how short life truly is helps us to keep these things in the proper perspective.

But also, in some amazing way, thinking of heaven also makes the little things matter *more*. I am loving people into eternity by pointing them toward God's love for them. I get to make them dinner again! I can discipline with fresh hope and a little more patience. I can endure a long and hard morning of homeschooling. I am not just dealing with annoying humans; I am loving immortal souls.

We want our kids to come home. We want them to like being home. We want to build a beautiful home. But ultimately, our temporary haven, at its best, points us toward our Real Home.

This gives me hope. Deep hope. When we fall flat on our faces (we will), it is not the end of the story. If we do everything wrong and seem to irrevocably screw up our job as mothers, it is not the end of the story. Someone stronger than us, more loving than us, is calling us Home. He is preparing a place for us. As we parent our children, God is parenting us. I want to build an amazing home, but even if I fail, it is okay. Home is waiting.

SUMMING IT UP

- We can't parent on our own; this is good news. God gives us the strength.
- A relational perspective asks in times of conflict, "What is the most important thing here? What is my end goal?"
- Forgive, forgive, forgive.

TALKING IT OVER

1. Who in your life is a model of grace? What can you learn from their example?
2. Are you someone who struggles to speak the truth at all or to speak the truth in love?
3. When has your parent or someone else showed you grace when you were difficult?

COMING HOME

Think of someone who forgave you. Tell them thank you.

One Family's Story: The Andersons

What a treat you're in for. I went to college with Kathy and Nathan, and their Facebook family updates are so beautiful they make me cry. I love the home they've built with their "little women"! Their five daughters are seven through sixteen years old.

Our parents gave us the priceless gift of warm, stable, loving, and fun homes where Christ was center; Mom and Dad were an inseparable, devoted team; and siblings were bound by traditions, laughter, biblical standards, and eternal identity. We have the privilege and responsibility to build on that legacy. When couples have not been given such a gift, they have the opportunity to forge a new legacy for their children and grandchildren.

Communication keeps us hemmed in as a family. It has always been important to us that we never lie to our kids, which builds deep trust. We strive to model quick repentance, apologies, and forgiveness to make it back to restored relationship without delay. When we see admirable, obedient, kind, or sacrificial behavior, we heap on the praise and encouragement. We say, "I love you" multiple times a day. Including our girls in as many discussions, decisions, conversations, and analyses as is appropriate gives them confidence in who we are and what we stand for.

Before we go out or host groups in our home, we encourage them with "You're an Anderson." It is meant to remind them that they represent Christ and our family to the outside world. They are trustworthy, they are willing to serve, they look for ways to be kind, they set a good example, and they lift others up. They are on the same team.

Our youngest daughter, Maeve, has intellectual and physical disabilities and is completely nonverbal. She is our special joy, and our love for her is wildly fierce and deeply tender. The challenges and joys we experience with and through her have shaped our family, knit us firmly together, and taught us all more than anything else could.

Daily, weekly, seasonal, and yearly traditions give the girls shared memories and things to look forward to. In our nightly prayer, we each lift up concerns, illnesses, fears, and thanksgiving to the Father. For our Sunday night "Wod-Fam-Choc-Sods" (*Adventures in Odyssey*, anyone?), Dad makes our secret recipe for glorified milkshakes and we toast to whatever happened that week or is coming up in the next.

Silliness and laughter are the underrated powerhouse of a close family. We want our home to be a place where we are all free to sing off-key, dance like weirdos, tell ridiculous jokes, and ask absurd questions without fear of mockery or ridicule. "It's just us!" we like to say. Playing family games, reading books aloud, and watching movies or shows *all together* leads to a bountiful harvest of favorite quotes and inside jokes that lighten challenging times and mend strained connections. Homeschooling gives us the invaluable gift of more time for all of it. Home is fun. Home is safe. Home is the best place on earth.

Acknowledgments

Todd: Patient, gracious, and steady—you complete me. Sam: I have always known God has big plans for you. It's fun to become friends with the amazing man you are becoming. Ty: My favorite middle child. Hardworking, thoughtful, and able to fix or find anything—we could not love you more. Ellie: My little sunshine and precious pumpkin. You are simply a delight.

Mom: Wherever you are is home. I love you always. Dad: Eternal optimist, enthusiastic cheerleader, generous giver—you make everything better. To my sisters, Jenny and Julie: Your homes feel like home to me. Thank you for feeding me (and our family), for encouraging me in all my crazy pursuits, and for being my very best friends. John: Remember that crazy time you sealed a business deal and gave our toddlers a shoebox full of dollar bills? That about sums you up. You're the best. Morgan, Julianne, and Helen: I hit the sister-in-law jackpot. I adore each of you. Carole and Doug: Every year that passes, I become more grateful for you. You gave us good roots, and I hope we make you proud.

Catherine, Tara, and Ashley: You prayed me along. So grateful for you. Mary DeMuth: You are sharp as a tack and insanely hardworking. Thank you, thank you for believing in me when I did not know if I believed in myself. Jillian: You are wise beyond your years. Thank you for wholeheartedly championing this project, and for being so sweet and gracious as you heard my ideas and made them much better. Donna: Not sure that I want to write a book without you; you were so kind as you cleaned up the editorial messes I created for you. Sarah Atkinson: Your "bad idea brainstorming" produced the title that made me cry. The Tyndale team: Gold stars from start to finish. It is an honor to be a Tyndale author.

To my Ablaze mastermind group: This book would not be without you. Thank you from the bottom of my heart. Monica Swanson: You always had just the right thing to say when I was discouraged.

This book was truly a community effort. A most heartfelt thanks to those who offered their stories, including: Paul and Laura Haggan, Jenn and John Fromke, Katie and Adam Collins, Kathy and Nathan Anderson, Shaun and Amy Turner, Lynn and Bruce Wray, Daniel and Brittany Brooker, Hudson and Catherine Belk, Jim and Carrie Luke, Natalie and Adam Renstrom, Graham and Katie Clark, Jamee Wetzel, Becky Hardenbrook, Jenny Haggan, Julie Chittock, Angela Howard, Lindsey Turner, and Lauren Verlander.

To my beta readers: Wow. I will never write a book without you again! Thank you for so generously sharing your traditions, opinions, and feedback. Particular thanks to Cathy, Jacqueline, Carla, Hannah, Ellen, Elisa, Christy, and Krysta—this is a better book because of the time each of you invested in it.

Finally, to my heavenly Father: I don't deserve any of this, least of all a home with You. How could I ever thank You?

Appendix 1

Note: For up-to-date links to resources mentioned in this book, visit jessicasmartt.com/favorites.

MOST EPIC LIST OF MEMORY-MAKING IDEAS EVER

Scenic

- Visit national parks or state parks.
- Go RV or tent camping.
- Visit Washington, DC.
- Attend a concert.
- Show up at a political rally, march, or fundraiser (great for encouraging civic involvement in older kids).
- View a sunrise at the beach.
- Rent a boat.
- Go on a horseback trail ride.
- Hike a waterfall (kids *love* water!).
- Take an epically long bike ride (if you're ever near Virginia, check out the Creeper Trail ride).
- View a hot-air balloon festival.
- Experience a Civil War battleground.
- Go on a mission trip together.

- Go to a rodeo.
- Try white water rafting, tubing, paddleboarding, or kayaking.
- Go skiing, snowboarding, or ice-skating.
- Visit Hawaii, Alaska, Costa Rica, or the Bahamas.
- Swim with dolphins.
- Drive across the country.
- Visit Disneyland (mixed feelings about this one . . . worth doing at least once, I would say).

Birthdays

- Have a "grandparents only" birthday party to spend intentional time with them—complete with piñata and games!
- Celebrate your kids' half-birthdays with half of a cupcake on half of a paper plate.
- Have kids follow a string to find their presents around the house.
- Write good qualities of the birthday person on a dry-erase board or chalkboard.
- Decorate with one balloon per year of their age above your child's bed.
- Hang streamers on your child's bedroom door for them to wake up to on their birthday.
- One year, instead of gifts, plan a trip for each child.
- Give your kids a book every year for birthdays, Valentine's, and Christmas. When they leave home, they'll have the makings of their own personal library.

St. Patrick's Day

- In addition to the yummy and traditional beef stew, shepherd's pie, or cheddar beer bread, add some spice to your day by putting green food dye in the toilet and placing cut-out leprechaun footprints next to it. Ha!

Easter

- Attend Ash Wednesday, Palm Sunday, Maundy Thursday, Good Friday, and Easter Sunday services. (If your church doesn't have these services, liturgical churches such as Anglican, Lutheran, or Presbyterian typically do.)
- Fast from something as a family during the weeks of Lent, except for Sundays!
- Create clues for the location of Easter baskets.
- Read a Lent devotional as a family. We love *Amon's Adventure* and *Make Room: A Child's Guide to Lent and Easter*.
- Make resurrection rolls or plant a resurrection garden.
- Observe Good Friday with a Mediterranean meal, eaten on the floor as Jesus and His disciples would have done.
- Stream Andrew Peterson's *Resurrection Letters* albums.
- Consider observing a "quiet Holy Week" by fasting from music, TV, and movies.
- Keep the lights off on Good Friday.

Christmas

- Celebrate St. Lucia's Day on December 13 by having the oldest daughter make breakfast in bed for the other members of the family.
- Drive around to look at Christmas lights—have a competition for which side of the car has the better lights.
- Polar Express surprise: put a ticket under your kids' pillows. Send them to bed, and when they find the ticket, tell them they are actually getting in the car, looking at lights, and drinking hot cocoa!
- Surprise-rake or -shovel someone's yard on Christmas morning before opening presents.
- Have a cookie-making day during the Christmas season!

- Celebrate Advent as a family: light candles in your home and have family dinners on Sundays during Advent season.
- Mom and Dad have a Christmas brunch date, then go shopping together.
- Plan a mother-daughter Christmas tea.
- See *The Nutcracker* together, then go to lunch.
- Listen to Handel's *Messiah* and Andrew Peterson's *Behold the Lamb of God.*
- Instead of many gifts on Christmas morning, put a gift in the kids' stockings on St. Nicholas Day, and then observe the Twelve Days of Christmas, giving one gift each day from Christmas to January 5.

New Year's

- Have a movie marathon or a game night marathon.
- Plan a fondue meal where you have to answer a question about the last year before you take a bite.
- Have a family sleepover.

Winter

- Celebrate winter solstice with hot cider and a fire.
- Buy a cheap blow-up hot tub to enjoy as a family.
- Sing at an assisted-living center for Valentine's Day.
- Cut out Valentine's hearts and write adjectives that each of your kids display. Put the hearts on their breakfast plates!
- Run a family "March Madness" bracket with prizes for the winners and (funny) consequences for the losers of each match.
- Track and cheer for the Iditarod Trail Sled Dog Race in early March. You can each pick a dog and see who wins!

Spring

- Celebrate May Day by bringing in flowers for your table.
- Let the person who sees the first robin of spring choose a dessert to make for dinner.

Summer

- Get a cake that says, "School's out for summer!" to enjoy on the last day of school, or have a pool party or water gun fight.
- Pick strawberries together and make jam or strawberry shortcake.
- Have a neighborhood or family summer Olympics, with events like mini-triathlon, jump rope, water balloon toss, trivia, and ice cream eating contest.
- Celebrate the Fourth of July by watching a Christmas movie (Christmas in July!) and having a pie party where everyone brings a pie, complete with judges and ribbons.[1] You can also listen to different versions of the national anthem or other patriotic songs, have a watermelon seed spitting contest, or make homemade ice cream.
- Have a summer reading contest with your family (and another family, if you want!). If you read the determined number of books, you get a collective prize, like a trip to an amusement park.

Fall

- Celebrate Martin Luther on Reformation Day. Have German food, bob for apples, and read or sing "A Mighty Fortress Is Our God."
- Have apple pie on the first chilly day.

- Go apple picking and have an apple-baking contest for which each person makes a unique apple dish.
- Carve pumpkins and text pictures to friends to have them vote on the winner.
- Have a back-to-school breakfast with each child to discuss what they're excited or nervous about for the coming school year.
- If you homeschool, have a NOT-back-to-school day. Wear your pajamas and drink hot chocolate as you wave the school bus by.

Appendix 2

FAMILY BONDING IDEAS

Thanks to my readers for many of these fun ideas.

At-Home Family Bonding Ideas

- Date night with a twist: one parent and one child go on a "date." Everyone else makes the meal for them.[1]
- Kids plan and make dinner: they pick a recipe, shop as a family, then prepare, with supervision as needed.
- Mom's diner: create a menu for kids to pick their items.
- Unbirthday party: buy streamers, balloons, cake with candles, a small present for everyone . . . only it's no one's birthday![2]
- Happy mail Mondays: write cards or letters with your kids to send to friends/family.
- Ice cream bracket: buy two flavors at a time and vote for the winner until you go from the "sweet sixteen" to the final favorite.
- Recreate board games or video games in real life, with your kids acting out the game pieces.
- Baking contests: give each of your kids two unique ingredients and see what they come up with.

- Sewing/quilting
- Nature study (books and documentaries)
- Family pizza night (make your own)
- Summer snow cone night
- Luau every summer

Out-of-the-Home Family Bonding Ideas

- Go paddleboarding.
- Attend an outdoor concert.
- Go to a fancy restaurant.
- Geocache.
- Play pickleball.
- Go for a bike ride.
- Watch a favorite sports team.
- Go kayaking.
- Visit a food truck festival.
- Go golfing.
- Visit a museum.
- Go camping.
- Go to the beach.
- Go fishing.
- Do some gardening.
- Go sledding.
- Play family T-ball.
- Shop at tag sales.
- Take a family hike or nature walk.
- Have a movie night in the backyard.
- Visit a Saturday morning farmers market.
- Pack a lunch and have a picnic before hitting a local trail, park, or garden.
- Set out buckets of mini marshmallows in the backyard for a marshmallow fight.

Appendix 3

JESSICA'S RECOMMENDED READING

Parenting

Boy Mom, Monica Swanson
The Collapse of Parenting, Leonard Sax
Hold On to Your Kids, Gordon Neufeld and Gabor Maté
Loving the Little Years, Rachel Jankovic
Mere Motherhood and *Beyond Mere Motherhood*, Cindy Rollins
Mother and Son, Emerson Eggerichs
Parenting, Paul David Tripp
The 7 Habits of Highly Effective Families, Stephen R. Covey
Simplicity Parenting, Kim John Payne with Lisa M. Ross
What Is a Family?, Edith Schaeffer
The Whole and Healthy Family, Jodi Mockabee

Marriage

The Empowered Wife, Laura Doyle
The Mystery of Marriage, Mike Mason

Faith

Habits of the Household, Justin Whitmel Earley
Heavenly Minded Mom, Katie Bennett

The Hiding Place, Corrie ten Boom
A Praying Life, Paul E. Miller

Homemaking

Decluttering at the Speed of Life, Dana K. White
Eve in Exile, Rebekah Merkle
Keeping House, Margaret Kim Peterson
Simplified Organization, Mystie Winckler
Sink Reflections, Marla Cilley

Hospitality

First We Have Coffee, Margaret Jensen
The Gospel Comes with a House Key, Rosaria Butterfield
Just Open the Door, Jen Schmidt
Soup Night Slapdashery, Rebekah Merkle

Celebrating

The Lifegiving Home, Sally Clarkson and Sarah Clarkson
Sacred Seasons, Danielle Hitchen
A Saint a Day, Meredith Hinds
Treasuring God in Our Traditions, Noël Piper

Notes

INTRODUCTION: LEGACY

1. John 14:2-3, NKJV.
2. *Oxford English Dictionary*, s.v. "legacy," accessed June 2024, https://www.oed.com/dictionary/legacy_n.
3. Kim John Payne, "We Underestimate the Power of Family," interview by Ginny Yurich, host, *The 1000 Hours Outside Podcast*, episode 1KHO 67, August 10, 2022, https://podcasts.apple.com/us/podcast/1kho-67-we-underestimate-the-power-of-family-kim/id1448210728?i=1000575715229.

CHAPTER 1: HONESTY

1. Jennifer Pepito, *Habits for a Sacred Home: 9 Practices from History to Anchor and Restore Modern Families* (Bethany House, 2024), 66.
2. Greg McKeown, *Essentialism: The Disciplined Pursuit of Less* (Crown Business, 2014), 31.
3. McKeown, 149.
4. See Mark 12:30-31.
5. Paul David Tripp, *Parenting: 14 Gospel Principles That Can Radically Change Your Family* (Crossway, 2016), 37.
6. See 2 Corinthians 12:9.

CHAPTER 2: PERSPECTIVE

1. Cindy Rollins, *Morning Time: A Liturgy of Love* (Blue Sky Daisies, 2021).
2. Rebekah Merkle, *Eve in Exile: The Restoration of Femininity* (Canon Press, 2016), 159.
3. Mystie Winckler, *Simplified Organization: Learn to Love What Must Be Done* (Convivial Press, 2023).
4. Amanda Reill, "A Simple Way to Make Better Decisions," *Harvard Business Review*, December 5, 2023, https://hbr.org/2023/12/a-simple-way-to-make-better-decisions.

5. See Galatians 6:7.
6. See 3 John 1:4.

CHAPTER 3: AUTHORITY

1. See Romans 13:1-2, for example.
2. Christian Dashiell, "'Elephant Parenting' Is the Healthiest Parenting Style—If You Avoid These 4 Mistakes," Fatherly, updated February 20, 2024, https://www.fatherly.com/parenting/elephant-parenting-healthiest-parenting-style-avoid-mistakes.
3. Leonard Sax, *The Collapse of Parenting: How We Hurt Our Kids When We Treat Them like Grown-Ups* (Basic Books, 2016), 140–141.
4. Jordan B. Peterson, *12 Rules for Life: An Antidote to Chaos* (Random House, 2018), 144.
5. Paul David Tripp, *Parenting: 14 Gospel Principles That Can Radically Change Your Family* (Crossway, 2016), 118.
6. Peterson, *12 Rules for Life*, 137.
7. Tripp, *Parenting*, 117.

CHAPTER 4: PARTNERSHIP

1. Timothy Keller with Kathy Keller, *The Meaning of Marriage: Facing the Complexities of Commitment with the Wisdom of God* (Riverhead Books, 2013), 144.
2. Herbert G. Lingren, "Strong Families," Cooperative Extension Service, University of Hawaiʻi at Mānoa, CF-13, July 1991, https://www.ctahr.hawaii.edu/oc/freepubs/pdf/CF-13.pdf (emphasis added); John DeFrain and Nick Stinnett, "Strong Families and Strong Farming Organizations: Is There a Connection?," Michigan Agricultural Experiment Station, Journal Article 12899, December 1988, https://ageconsearch.umn.edu/record/260101/files/Article07.pdf.
3. Eugene C. Roehlkepartain et al., "Building Strong Families: An In-Depth Report on a Preliminary Survey on What Parents Need to Succeed," YMCA of the USA and Search Institute, 2002, https://www.search-institute.org/wp-content/uploads/2018/02/2002BuildingStrongFamilies-InDepthReport.pdf.
4. Ellie Lisitsa, "The Four Horsemen: Criticism, Contempt, Defensiveness, and Stonewalling," The Gottman Institute, updated October 15, 2024, https://www.gottman.com/blog/the-four-horsemen-recognizing-criticism-contempt-defensiveness-and-stonewalling/.

CHAPTER 5: PRAYER

1. Rachel Wojo, *Desperate Prayers: Embracing the Power of Prayer in Life's Darkest Moments* (Skyhorse, 2024), 27.
2. See 1 Samuel 1:27-28.

3. Paul E. Miller, *A Praying Life: Connecting with God in a Distracting World* (NavPress, 2017), 47.
4. Cindy Rollins, *Beyond Mere Motherhood: Moms Are People Too* (Blue Sky Daisies, 2023), 44–45.
5. Joseph Medlicott Scriven, "What a Friend We Have in Jesus," 1855.
6. Miller, *Praying Life*. See chapter 29, "Keeping Track of the Story: Using Prayer Cards," for a description of his prayer card system.

CHAPTER 6: TIME

1. John DeFrain et al., *How Strong Families Manage Stress and Crisis* (University of Nebraska–Lincoln Extension HEF590, 2009), https://extensionpubs.unl.edu/publication/hef590/2010/pdf/view/hef590-2010.pdf.
2. Richard Innes, "Making Families Strong—Part Two," ACTS International, accessed October 26, 2024, https://www.actsweb.org/articles/article.php?i=737&d=2&c=3.
3. Nick Stinnett, quoted in Maria Krysan et al., *Research on Successful Families* (US Department of Health and Human Services, May 1990), https://aspe.hhs.gov/reports/research-successful-families-0.
4. Timothy Keller with Kathy Keller, *The Meaning of Marriage: Facing the Complexities of Commitment with the Wisdom of God* (Penguin, 2013), 160–161.
5. Edith Schaeffer, *What Is a Family?* (Baker, 1975), 201.
6. Schaeffer, 183.
7. Schaeffer, 194.
8. Marc Novicoff, "'It's Causing Them to Drop Out of Life': How Phones Warped Gen Z," *Politico Magazine*, March 24, 2024, https://www.politico.com/news/magazine/2024/03/24/the-anxious-generation-qa-00147880.
9. Novicoff, "'It's Causing Them to Drop Out.'"
10. Novicoff, "'It's Causing Them to Drop Out.'"
11. Aina Marzia, "Why Gen Z Won't Be Raising 'iPad Kids,'" The Daily Beast, March 18, 2024, https://www.thedailybeast.com/why-gen-z-wont-be-raising-ipad-kids.
12. Cindy Rollins, *Beyond Mere Motherhood: Moms Are People Too* (Blue Sky Daisies, 2023), 36.
13. "Benefits of Family Dinners," The Family Dinner Project, accessed November 20, 2024, https://thefamilydinnerproject.org/about-us/benefits-of-family-dinners/.
14. "The Benefits of the Family Table," American College of Pediatricians, February 2021, https://acpeds.org/position-statements/the-benefits-of-the-family-table.

15. Leonard Sax, *The Collapse of Parenting: How We Hurt Our Kids When We Treat Them like Grown-Ups* (Basic Books, 2016), 110.

CHAPTER 7: CONNECTION

1. Be sure to check it out for lots more ideas about building a strong family! (Thomas Nelson, 2019.)
2. The prayer card system is described in chapter 29 of Miller's book *A Praying Life* (NavPress, 2017).
3. Gordon Neufeld and Gabor Maté, *Hold On to Your Kids: Why Parents Need to Matter More Than Peers* (Ballantine, 2006), 179.
4. Neufeld and Maté, 181–182.
5. Charles R. Swindoll, "8 Characteristics of a Healthy Family," Lifeway, January 1, 2014, https://www.lifeway.com/en/articles/eight-characteristics-of-a-healthy-family.
6. If you'd like a copy of this book, you can request it on my website, "Smartter" Each Day, http://smarttereachday.com/the-family-question-book-250-questions/.
7. Sally Lloyd Jones, *The Jesus Storybook Bible: Every Story Whispers His Name* (Zonderkidz, 2007), 36.
8. J. R. R. Tolkien, *The Fellowship of the Ring: Being the First Part of the Lord of the Rings* (Houghton Mifflin, 2012), 36.
9. Gary Chapman, *The 5 Love Languages: The Secret to Love That Lasts* (Northfield, 2010). For an overview of the love languages, visit this site: "What Are the 5 Love Languages?," Love Languages, accessed October 30, 2024, https://5lovelanguages.com/learn.
10. James 1:5.
11. 1 Corinthians 13:4.
12. Michaeleen Doucleff, *Hunt, Gather, Parent: What Ancient Cultures Can Teach Us About the Lost Art of Raising Happy, Helpful Little Humans* (Avid Reader Press, 2022), 16.
13. Doucleff, 76.
14. Doucleff, 87.
15. Sissy Goff, *Raising Worry-Free Girls: Helping Your Daughter Feel Braver, Stronger, and Smarter in an Anxious World* (Bethany House, 2019), 126.
16. Rachel Jankovic, *Loving the Little Years: Motherhood in the Trenches* (Canon Press, 2010), 29–30.
17. 2 Timothy 4:2, ESV.
18. Neufeld and Maté, *Hold On to Your Kids*, 189.
19. Neufeld and Maté, 194–195.

CHAPTER 8: MEMORIES

1. If you enjoy this chapter, be sure to check out that first book: Jessica Smartt, *Memory-Making Mom: Building Traditions That Breathe Life into Your Home* (Thomas Nelson, 2019).

2. Edith Schaeffer, *What Is a Family?* (Baker, 1997), 199.
3. Justin Whitmel Earley, *Habits of the Household: Practicing the Story of God in Everyday Family Rhythms* (Zondervan, 2021), 213.
4. For more information, visit the National Park Service website: "Every Kid Outdoors Program Provides Fourth Grade Students with Free Entrance to Public Lands," National Park Service, September 4, 2019, https://www.nps.gov/orgs/1207/every-kid-outdoors-program-provides-fourth-grade-students-with-free-entrance-to-public-lands.htm.
5. Erin Odom, text message to author, October 19, 2024.
6. Erin Odom, *You Can Stay Home with Your Kids! 100 Tips, Tricks, and Ways to Make It Work on a Budget* (Zondervan, 2018), 110–113.
7. Karen Formost, "How to Celebrate 'Jolabokaflod'—the Icelandic 'Book Flood' Tradition!," *Read Watch Go* (blog), January 17, 2021, https://www.readwatchgo.com/blog/jolabokaflod.
8. Danielle Hitchen, *Sacred Seasons: A Family Guide to Center Your Year Around Jesus* (Harvest House, 2023), 20.
9. Hitchen, 40, 41, 44.
10. Hitchen, 64.
11. Hitchen, 80.
12. Hitchen, 112.
13. Phylicia Masonheimer, "How Our Family Celebrates All Saints Day," Every Woman a Theologian, accessed November 2, 2024, https://phyliciamasonheimer.com/how-our-family-celebrates-all-saints-day/.

CHAPTER 9: NEST

1. Charlotte Mason, *Home Education* (Wilder Publications, 2015), 9.
2. Mystie Winckler, *Simplified Organization: Learn to Love What Must Be Done* (Convivial Press, 2023), 165–166.
3. 2 Timothy 2:15.
4. Kim John Payne, *Simplicity Parenting: Using the Extraordinary Power of Less to Raise Calmer, Happier, and More Secure Kids* (Ballantine Books, 2010), 18.
5. Justin Whitmel Earley, *Habits of the Household: Practicing the Story of God in Everyday Family Rhythms* (Zondervan, 2021), 4.
6. Earley, 16.
7. Rebekah Merkle, *Eve in Exile: The Restoration of Femininity* (Canon Press, 2016), 157.
8. Merkle, 158.

CHAPTER 10: ROOTS

1. Robert Kourik, "Roots Demystified: The Amazing Unseen Things Roots Do," interview by Joe Lamp'l, *The Joe Gardener Show with Joe Lamp'l*, podcast, episode 215, July 1, 2021, https://joegardener.com/podcast/roots-demystified/.

2. Bonnie Balis, "A Plant's Health Issues Are Usually Root-Related," *Progress-Index*, June 19, 2016, https://www.progress-index.com/story/lifestyle/home-garden/2016/06/19/a-plant-s-health-issues/27634687007/.
3. Susan D. Day and P. Eric Wiseman, "At the Root of It," *Arborist News*, December 2009, 20, https://wwv.isa-arbor.com/education/resources/educ_Portal_RootGrowth_AN.pdf.
4. Justin Whitmel Earley, *Habits of the Household: Practicing the Story of God in Everyday Family Rhythms* (Zondervan, 2021), 32.
5. Kim John Payne, "We Underestimate the Power of Family," interview by Ginny Yurich, host, *The 1000 Hours Outside Podcast*, episode 1KHO 67, August 10, 2022, YouTube, https://www.youtube.com/watch?v=X4zpMgto_dc.
6. Adapted from Stephen R. Covey, *The 7 Habits of Highly Effective Families: Creating a Nurturing Family in a Turbulent World*, rev. ed. (St. Martins Essentials, 2022), 78–84.
7. Leonard Sax, *The Collapse of Parenting: How We Hurt Our Kids When We Treat Them like Grown-Ups* (Basic Books, 2016), 107.

CHAPTER 11: LOYALTY

1. Kim John Payne and Luis Fernando Llosa, *Emotionally Resilient Tweens and Teens: Empowering Your Kids to Navigate Bullying, Teasing, and Social Exclusion* (Shambhala Publications, 2022), 13–14.
2. Payne and Llosa, 13.
3. See Galatians 6:2.
4. Payne and Llosa, *Emotionally Resilient Tweens and Teens*, 14.

CHAPTER 12: FRIENDSHIP

1. Clare M. Stocker et al., "Sibling Relationships in Older Adulthood: Links with Loneliness and Well-Being," *Journal of Family Psychology* 34, no. 2 (August 15, 2020): 175–185, https://www.ncbi.nlm.nih.gov/pmc/articles/PMC7012710/.
2. Stocker et al., "Sibling Relationships in Older Adulthood."
3. Nicholeen Peck, *Parenting: A House United; Changing Children's Hearts and Behaviors by Teaching Self-Government* (Teaching Self-government, 2009), 19.
4. Jessica Smartt, *Let Them Be Kids: Adventure, Boredom, Innocence, and Other Gifts Children Need* (Thomas Nelson, 2020).

CHAPTER 13: GRACE

1. See Proverbs 10:19; 13:3; 21:23, NKJV.
2. Herbert G. Lingren, "Strong Families," Cooperative Extension Service, University of Hawai'i at Mānoa, CF-13, July 1991, https://www.ctahr.hawaii.edu/oc/freepubs/pdf/CF-13.pdf; and John DeFrain and Nick

Stinnett, "Strong Families and Strong Farming Organizations: Is There a Connection?," Michigan Agricultural Experiment Station, Journal Article 12899, December 1988, https://ageconsearch.umn.edu/record/260101/files/Article07.pdf.

3. Charles R. Swindoll, "8 Characteristics of a Healthy Family," Lifeway, January 1, 2014, https://www.lifeway.com/en/articles/eight-characteristics-of-a-healthy-family.
4. See Hebrews 12:15.
5. Gordon Neufeld and Gabor Maté, *Hold On to Your Kids: Why Parents Need to Matter More Than Peers* (Ballantine, 2006), 179.
6. Corrie ten Boom, with John Sherrill and Elizabeth Sherrill, *The Hiding Place* (Chosen Books, 1984), 248.
7. John 14:2, NKJV.
8. See Psalm 90:12.

APPENDIX 1

1. Contributed by a reader in my Facebook group (@Jessica Smartt, author), https://www.facebook.com/SmarterEachDay/.

APPENDIX 2

1. From the "Mere Motherhood" Facebook group.
2. From the "Mere Motherhood" Facebook group.

About the Author

JESSICA SMARTT is the author of *Memory-Making Mom* and *Let Them Be Kids*. She lives in sunny North Carolina on a family farm with horses, chickens, and an ever-increasing number of cats. She and her husband, Todd, have three kids whom they homeschool. Jessica loves bike rides, spinach quiche, a clean kitchen, being warm, national parks, and food that anyone else made.